THE ORVIS® GUIDE TO

THE ESSENTIAL AMERICAN FLIES

THE ORVIS

GUIDE TO

THE ESSENTIAL AMERICAN FLIES

HOW TO TIE THE MOST SUCCESSFUL FRESHWATER AND SALTWATER PATTERNS

TOM ROSENBAUER

UNIVERSE

To my son, Brett,
my fly-tying buddy, whose little desk
is right next to mine, and who constantly
amazes me with his creativity.

Published by Universe Publishing
A Division of Rizzoli International Publications, Inc.
300 Park Avenue South
New York, NY 10010
www.rizzoliusa.com

© 2011 Tom Rosenbauer

All photographs © Tom Rosenbauer, except the following:

p. 8: Courtesy of Lefty Kreh; p. 10: © David Philipps; p. 17: © Emily Whitlock;
p. 29: Courtesy of Eric Troth; p. 37: Courtesy of Trout Unlimited;
p. 67: Courtesy of The American Museum of Fly Fishing; p. 79: Courtesy of Craig Matthews;
p. 87: Courtesy of Randall Kaufmann; p. 117: © John Randolf; p. 149: © Barry Beck;
p. 159: Courtesy of Bob Clouser; p. 171: Courtesy of Lefty Kreh;
p. 189: Courtesy of Bob Popovics; p. 201: Courtesy of Ken J. McLeod

Project Editor: Candice Fehrman
Book Design: Lori S. Malkin
Text and Photography: Tom Rosenbauer
Fly Illustrations: James Daley

2011 2012 2013 2014 / 10 9 8 7 6 5 4 3 2 1

Printed in China

ISBN-13: 978-0-7893-2269-2

Library of Congress Catalog Control Number: 2011921540

Acknowledgments

I was fortunate enough to be able to speak directly with the originators of many of these iconic American fly patterns, and for that honor I am grateful. Thank you to Bob Clouser, Bob Popovics, Craig Matthews, Dave Whitlock, Enrico Puglisi, Lefty Kreh, and Randall Kaufmann for your tolerance of my pestering and frequent questions. I also had the great pleasure of spending the day with the late Art Flick back in the 1980s, and revisiting my interview from that day was a pleasant reminder of my time with that warm and generous man.

I'd also like to thank Eric Troth for sharing his insight on his dad and on the development of the Elk Hair Caddis, and Ken J. McLeod, who was very helpful in providing information on his father and the Skykomish Sunrise, as well as sharing photos of his father's fly box with me.

Ed Schroeder and Randall Kaufmann helped me get a better sense of Doug Prince and his development of the Prince nymph than I could get from any written history of California fly fishing. Cathy Ransier from The Book Mailer was helpful in filling in background information on Antron yarn and on Gary LaFontaine's research, and Barry Beck gave me some great firsthand information on Russell Blessing and the development of the Woolly Bugger.

Trying to get just the right materials for these patterns was often a challenge, and I'd like to thank Shawn Brillon, Bill Keough, Craig Matthews, and Enrico Puglisi for their patience and generosity with my pestering for specific colors and textures of all kinds of feathers, hairs, and yarns.

I want to extend a very special thank you to T. L. Lauerman of the Wapsi Fly Company, not only for his help with inside information on the sourcing and development of fly-tying materials, but also for his frequent FedEx packages of materials just in time for my weekend tying and photography sessions.

A huge thank you to my editors, Candice Fehrman and Jim Muschett, for their patience and cheerful tolerance of my last-minute photos and chapters, and for their amazing skill at organizing this complex book into a thing of beauty. People who complain about the impersonal nature of publishing and long for the old days when editors were truly helpful and considerate have never worked with these two.

To my wife, Robin, for her support of this project, which seemed to go on forever, and for her understanding and cheerful acceptance of many weekends where family activities were cut short by my stressing out about hitting deadlines.

And to my son, Brett, who inspires me with his creativity at the fly-tying vise and makes me laugh when things don't go just right.

Table of Contents

5 ■ Acknowledgments

8 ■ Foreword by Lefty Kreh

9 ■ Introduction by Tom Rosenbauer

Dry Flies

16 ■ Dave's Hopper
Sidebar: Oak-Mottled Turkey
Pattern Variations:
Joe's (Michigan) Hopper and
Letort Hopper

28 ■ Elk Hair Caddis
Sidebar: Hare's Ear Fur
Pattern Variation: X-Caddis

36 ■ Griffith's Gnat
Sidebar: Tying with Peacock Herl
Pattern Variation:
Hi-Vis Griffith's Gnat

44 ■ Parachute Adams
Sidebar: Mixing Hackles
Pattern Variations: Traditional
Adams and Parachute Hare's Ear

56 ■ Red Quill
Sidebar: Stripped Hackle Stem Bodies
Pattern Variation: Dun Variant

66 ■ Royal Wulff
Sidebar:
Choosing Wings for Visible Flies
Pattern Variations:
Royal Trude and Royal Humpy

78 ■ Sparkle Dun
Sidebar:
Selecting Hair for Sparkle Duns
Pattern Variations: Haystack and
PMD Comparadun

86 ■ Stimulator
Sidebar: How to Choose Elk Hair
Pattern Variations: Rubber-Leg
Crystal Stimulator (Fluorescent
Green), Foamulator (Black),
and Royal Stimulator

96 ■ Yellow Humpy
Sidebar:
Hackles for Big Dry Flies
Pattern Variations: Green Humpy
and Orange Humpy

Nymphs

108 ■ American Pheasant Tail
Sidebar: Working with Beads
Pattern Variations: Beadhead
Pheasant Tail and Original
Frank Sawyer Pheasant Tail

116 ■ LaFontaine's
Deep Sparkle Pupa
Sidebar: Antron, Z-Lon, and
LaFontaine's Sparkle Yarn
Pattern Variations:
Dark Gray Deep Sparkle Pupa
and Emergent Sparkle Pupa

124 ■ Prince
Sidebar:
   Wet Fly and Nymph Hackle
Pattern Variations: Dark Lord
   and The Fly Formerly Known
   as Prince

Streamers

136 ■ Muddler Minnow
Sidebar: Spinning Deer Hair for
   Muddler Heads
Pattern Variations: White
   Marabou Muddler and Yellow
   Conehead Marabou Muddler

148 ■ Woolly Bugger
Sidebar: Choosing Marabou
Pattern Variations: Crystal Bugger,
   Black Tunghead Woolly Bugger,
   and Egg-Sucking Leech

Saltwater Flies

158 ■ Clouser Deep Minnow
Sidebar:
   Natural and Synthetic Materials
Pattern Variations: Half-and-Half
   and Ultra Hair Albie Clouser

164 ■ Crazy Charlie
Sidebar: Eyes for Bonefish Flies
Pattern Variations: Christmas
   Island Special and Gotcha

170 ■ Lefty's Deceiver
Sidebar:
   Hackles for Saltwater Flies
Pattern Variations:
   Black Lefty's Deceiver and
   Cockroach Lefty's Deceiver

178 ■ Peanut Butter
Sidebar: Dealing with Fine
   Synthetic Hair
Pattern Variations: Floating
   Baitfish and Mangrove Baitfish

188 ■ Surf Candy
Sidebar:
   Using Resins in Saltwater Flies
Pattern Variations:
   Deep Candy and
   Full-Dress Surf Candy

Steelhead

200 ■ Skykomish Sunrise
Sidebar:
   Styles of Steelhead Flies
Pattern Variations:
   Skykomish Dark and
   Trey Combs Skykomish Sunrise

207 ■ Index

Foreword

Talk to any well-traveled and widely experienced fly fisherman about his observations concerning great local fishermen he encounters and you'll almost always hear the same comment: "These successful anglers use relatively few patterns to catch most of their fish."

Upon further examination, it's probably true that many of the patterns successful anglers choose

have been around a long time. For example, almost every experienced dry-fly fisherman carries the Adams and Elk Hair Caddis in various sizes and probably has a Pheasant Tail and Prince nymph. There are solid reasons why time-tested patterns are in common use in fresh- and saltwater—they have produced for years. Many of these favored flies can be fished in several different ways. Just one example is the Woolly Bugger, which can be tied in a huge number of variations. It can be dead drifted as a helpless fish fly larvae or hellgrammite, or thrown across the stream and fished as a wet fly, or even zipped along like an escaping minnow.

If you are a fly tier, you'll really appreciate this book. Tom Rosenbauer selects for the reader 20 effective patterns and gives a bit of history about each fly and its originator. He offers a recipe for each pattern, followed by superb photos showing step-by-step tying instructions. The text explains how to select and prepare the proper materials for each pattern, as well as special tying tricks. Each chapter also includes popular variations of the pattern.

If you are not an experienced fly fisherman and you walk into a fly shop to select a fly, the immense number of patterns can be overwhelming. No problem. In this book, Tom Rosenbauer has chosen 20 patterns that have produced over the years. Buy these, learn how and when to use them, and you almost certainly will catch more fish.

—LEFTY KREH

Introduction

Fly fishing is pretty one-dimensional without an appreciation of its saga. How did we get here and why do we go through silly antics to catch a fish with a feathered hook when it is so much more efficient to toss a worm or live minnow into the depths? Many fly fishers feel that flies are an especially intriguing part of this narrative because the lures we use to deceive fish were created by human hands—crafted from a mixture of natural and synthetic materials—and are still being made by hand today, even when produced in large commercial factories.

How did we end up with such a vast number of flies, and why are some more popular than others? The answer to the first part of the question is easy—we love to create new flies. Anyone can do it. Sometimes the creation of a new fly arises from the mind of someone who thinks around corners and bypasses the straight-line logic that most of us use. Many fly patterns arise from a problem-solving process, because problem solving is at the essence of fly fishing—from finding a fish to determining how to make a cast to attempting to land a fish without losing it. Bead eyes on bonefish flies. Lead eyes on streamers. Deer-hair heads on sculpin imitations. Epoxy on baitfish flies. Elk hair on caddis flies. Where would we be without these innovations born out of trying to solve a problem? The flies in this book truly revolutionized the way we look at flies today.

As for the second part of the question, it's easy to be cynical and suggest that new flies are just marketing—somebody writes a magazine article, the public clamors for the fly pattern the author wrote about, and tackle shops and catalogs make the fly pattern available to anyone with a few extra bucks. Marketing can account for short-term popularity of a fly pattern, but those flies that have been occupying the front row in little aluminum boxes for more than 20 years have not survived for this reason; that is, not any more than marketing explains the long-term popularity of songs like Beethoven's Third or the Beatles's "She Loves You," which are still being played on MP3 players today. They just work. You can pick the songs apart and determine a few elements that make them special, but the particular combination of chords, harmony, rhythm, and orchestration in a piece of music that has endured makes them timeless, just as a specific mixture of fur, feathers, tinsel, synthetics, and the precise order and manner they are tied to a hook makes a fly that is still highly effective 50 years from its first use. Even though we learn more about fly fishing every year and fly-tying materials and fly tiers keep getting better, it's hard to improve on a fly pattern like the Royal Wulff. And many have tried.

In developing this collection of essential, iconic American flies, I had to make some judgment calls. All of the flies included here were developed at least 20 years ago, and all have been popular since their development and have been prominent in catalogs and fly boxes. I picked 20 years as an arbitrary figure, but I think that being at the top of the hit parade for two decades ensures that a fly pattern has risen above the hype and is not only effective, but will probably be important for at least another generation.

The fly-tying patterns in this book were created by a number of processes. The Woolly Bugger may be nothing but a Woolly Worm (an ancient pattern) with a marabou tail, but the sum of those two elements is so much more than its parts, and it took Russell Blessing to come up with the winning combination. Fly tiers before Gary LaFontaine had tried to imitate caddis pupae, but no one put the thousands of hours into underwater observation, experimentation with patterns, and a quest for exactly the right materials to imitate one single bug that he did. And probably no one has since.

I feel that before one can truly arrive as a fly tier you have to study the work of the masters, if only to realize that the fabulous new fly-tying technique you dreamed up last night was actually being used by Art Flick back in the 1940s. For the patterns in this book, I tried to go right to the source— to the originator if possible, and if the originator was no longer alive, then to his books or descendents or fishing buddies—to find out exactly how he created the fly. Here's a good example of why: I have been tying Clouser Minnows since I first read about them in the 1980s and they've worked well for me. However, until I talked to Bob Clouser about how he ties the pattern and really studied every turn of thread he makes, I didn't realize I was tying the fly all wrong. My flies were too broad at the head, they had no flowing taper, and the eyes were placed too far forward. These are subtle differences in the tying steps, but taken together they make my recent Clouser Minnows almost a new species from the old ones in my box.

I limited the patterns to American inventions to give the book better focus, which introduced conundrums of its own, especially with nymphs. The Gold-Ribbed Hare's Ear nymph is at the top of nearly everyone's favorite flies list, and even Lefty Kreh, after reading the book prior to writing his foreword, asked me, "Why no Hare's Ear nymph? I use it more than anything." But in digging into the origin of the Gold-Ribbed Hare's Ear, I couldn't determine with certainty that it's an American pattern. A wet fly with the same materials we use for our modern Gold-Ribbed Hare's Ear has been in use for hundreds of years, and when nymphs became popular in England in the early 20th century, both Frederick

Halford and G. E. M. Skues took the traditional wet-fly pattern and created a nymph from it. I don't know for sure if it's the exact same pattern we use today, but I believe it has not changed much over 100 years. Even the beadhead variation of the Hare's Ear nymph was probably used in Europe in the 1980s before Americans began putting beads on every nymph imaginable.

The Pheasant Tail nymph was another judgment call. Although the Pheasant Tail is absolutely a British invention, perfected by Frank Sawyer on the River Avon, I feel that Al Troth's variation, which changed not only some of the materials used but also the basic silhouette of the fly, is truly a new fly pattern. That he chose not to name it the Troth's Special is a testament to his humility.

You'll notice I did not include any large foam dry flies in this collection of essential flies. Nearly every trout angler uses some type of large foam dry fly today, and there are a couple of patterns, like the Chernobyl Ant or the Turck's Tarantula, that almost fit my criteria for essential American flies, but I think the jury is still out on which foam dry fly will rise to the top. Each year a vast crop of new ones hits the marketplace, and I think we need another few years to decide which ones are classics. That's a subject for a volume two of this book somewhere down the road.

It's part of the creative process of fly tying to develop your own fly patterns, but I think most tiers are better served by trying to imitate the classics shown here, especially if your time at the fly-tying vise is limited. By studying the techniques of the masters, you'll see what processes went into making these flies groundbreaking, and you'll learn most of the valuable techniques used to create the many variations you see every year in the new fly offerings on Web sites and in catalogs. For example, studying how Enrico Puglisi layers and shapes his materials will give you ideas on how to use new synthetic materials in the same manner to get a different effect.

In my 45 years of fly tying, I've invented hundreds of new fly patterns. About a half-dozen of them were worth adding to my fly box or telling friends about, and none of them have come even close to making the grade for the fly patterns I've shown you here. Since my time at the vise is limited, just as yours probably is, every year I spend more and more time perfecting the way I tie the essential patterns, with an occasional side trip when I experiment with a slightly different material or technique. I expect you will get more out of your fly tying by learning how to tie the Clouser Minnow perfectly and then experimenting with color variations than by dreaming up something like Joe's Killer Mill River Parachute Emerger.

Dry Flies

Dave Whitlock of Mountain Home, Arkansas, has been one of the top innovators in the fly-fishing world for many decades. As an angler, teacher, writer, artist, photographer, conservationist, fly tier, and tackle tinkerer, there are not many aspects of modern fly fishing he has not touched. One of his most lasting innovations is a grasshopper pattern that is by far the most popular hopper imitation throughout the world, the Dave's Hopper.

Fly tiers began to think seriously about imitating grasshoppers in the middle of the 20th century, and although fly catalogs of 100 years ago showed grasshopper flies, they were either too crude or so slavishly realistic that the resulting fly was too stiff, didn't float well, and didn't behave like a live grasshopper on the water. The best early imitation was the Michigan Hopper, developed by Art Winnie in the 1940s and still popular today. But the Michigan Hopper is not a great floater; it doesn't land much like a grasshopper and it doesn't float like the natural. Using hackle and wet fly-style turkey wings, it was just a slight modification of the aquatic insect imitations of its day, with an attempt to shoehorn in the look of a grasshopper. For decades, though, it was so popular with legendary outdoor writer Joe Brooks that it became known as Joe's Hopper.

In the 1950s, fly fishers realized they could grease up their

■ Dave Whitlock

Hook
2XL dry fly or 3XL nymph hook,
sizes 4–12

Thread
Yellow 6/0 for body, gray or white
3/0 for head

Tail
Red elk hock, or coarse red hair at the
bottom of a red-dyed bucktail

Rib
Clipped brown hackle

Body
Yellow polypropylene yarn

Underwing
Yellow deer body hair or coarse hair from
the bottom of a yellow-dyed bucktail

Overwing
Oak-mottled turkey wing quill section,
stiffened

Kicker Legs
Knotted section of ringneck pheasant
tail fibers

Collar
Natural deer body hair

Head
Natural deer body hair, clipped to
rectangular shape

hopper. Schwiebert's Letort Hopper is a simple yet deadly pattern, especially good for tiny early season hoppers, when the more artistic dressings are too complicated for a size 14 hook. It is still a widely used fly throughout the world.

Dave Whitlock began fishing the trout streams of the Rocky Mountains in the 1950s. He remembers his first trip, when he was 16 years old, because while he was fishing a tributary of the Yellowstone River, he found the hopper-eating trout to be so finicky that he had to resort to live grasshoppers to catch them. Frustrated, he made a visit to Dan Bailey's Fly Shop in Livingston, Montana, and Bailey recommended the Joe's Hopper, which worked well for Whitlock. He wasn't totally satisfied, however. A few years later, Whitlock met Joe Brooks, and Brooks complained that the Joe's Hopper kept twisting his leader so he had resorted to a greased Muddler Minnow. "That didn't look too great to my artistic eye," Whitlock said, "so I decided to work on my own imitation, which resulted in the Dave's Hopper, which I first

■ In meadow streams in late summer, a Dave's Hopper may be the only dry fly you will need.

Muddler Minnow streamer with Mucilin line dressing and the Muddler, with its turkey wings and hollow deer-hair head, did a reasonable job of imitating both the look of a grasshopper on the water and the way one lands with a tiny splash. A young Ernest Schwiebert took Ed Shenk's Letort Cricket, a staple of Pennsylvania spring-creek anglers, and modified the dressing to look like a

Oak-Mottled Turkey

Oak-mottled turkey secondary feathers are a fly-tying staple. Nothing matches the mottled color of hopper wings better. In fact, I remember fishing when I was a kid with a plastic realistic grasshopper imitation that had a body and legs made of soft plastic, yet the wings were made from mottled turkey feathers sealed in some type of glue.

Many fly patterns besides grasshopper imitations also call for mottled turkey wing. Many wet-fly patterns, the Muddler Minnow, and a great number of nymphs use it for wing cases. Yet really nice oak-mottled turkey is hard to find, and when you do find it, the price is steep, especially when you consider how many secondary quills a turkey owns. According to T.L. Lauerman of the Wapsi Fly Company, the largest fly-tying material supplier in the world, most of the domestic turkeys we ate 30 years ago were darker birds with speckled wings that looked very much like wild turkeys. But diners objected to the dark spots on a turkey skin that were caused by the dark pinfeathers of the mottled domestic bird, so gradually this color variation was replaced with a pure white breed, where the pinfeathers blend into the skin. There are apparently only a few farms still raising the older mottled varieties, thus the scarcity of oak-mottled feathers.

Oak-mottled turkey comes in various shades, from an almost-white feather with fine brown speckling to very dark shades with strong dark brown bars. Most patterns call for the darker feather, especially for grasshopper patterns, so when buying these feathers through the mail ask for a darker shade if you have the option. The darker brown turkey tail feathers do not make good hopper wings. The feather is too stiff; when trying to roll it over the top of a hook, turkey tails will split.

One option is to use secondary feathers from a wild turkey. Although not as finely speckled as oak-mottled domestic turkey, wild turkey has strong barring and offers a nice dark shade. On a finished fly it's hard to distinguish from oak-mottled turkey. With wild turkeys getting more abundant every year in nearly every state, it's pretty easy to get enough secondary feathers from a single bird to last a lifetime. If you don't hunt yourself, ask around, as turkey hunters usually just throw the secondary feathers away, keeping only the tail fan, beard, and claws as trophies.

Feathers from turkey wings should come from the short side of the feather, usually the side where the fibers curve strongly in one direction. The fibers on the other side of the stem often have a compound curve so they are tough to shape into a hopper wing that looks pleasing. Save that side for wing cases on nymphs. Also, for durability and ease of handling, turkey wing quills used for hopper wings should be stiffened prior to use. There are many products that will work and all seem to be equally effective. Vinyl cement, Dave's Flexament, and Feather Tough are some of the types sold in fly shops. But clear acrylic sealers, sold in artist supply shops in a spray form, are quick and easy to use. Spray or wipe a thin coat of any of these preparations on the "back" side of the feather (the shiny or concave side) so that the natural texture of the feather shows on the top of the fly. Any treated feather should be allowed to dry for an hour or so before tying with it. It's not important to the fish, but as fly tiers we like our finished creations to look perfect!

■ On the right is a light mottled turkey quill, and in the center is a darker mottled turkey quill, the shade preferred for hoppers. On the left is a secondary quill from a wild turkey, which makes a fine substitute for hopper wings.

JOE'S (MICHIGAN) HOPPER

Hook: 2XL dry fly or 3XL nymph hook, sizes 4–12

Thread: Yellow 6/0

Tail: Red hackle fibers

Rib: Clipped brown hackle

Body: Yellow dubbing

Wing: Oak-mottled turkey wing quill sections, tied along both sides

Hackle: Brown and grizzly

LETORT HOPPER

Hook: 2XL dry fly or 3XL nymph hook, sizes 6–14

Thread: Yellow 6/0

Body: Pale yellow dubbing or angora yarn

Wing: Oak-mottled turkey wing quill section, tied flat over body

Collar: Deer hair

Head: Spun and trimmed deer hair

Note: All three of the hopper patterns in this chapter are also tied with gray, green, and orange bodies and heads to match grasshoppers of different shades. The Letort Hopper and Dave's Hopper are also tied in all black to imitate crickets.

used about 1962." The original pattern had no kicker legs, but Wyoming fly tier Jay Buchner suggested that Whitlock add legs made of trimmed hackle stems. Later, another tier, Dick Alf, was the first to use the knotted pheasant tail legs used today. The pheasant tail legs are not as stiff as the hackle stems and result in a more aerodynamic fly.

There has been a recent craze of tying grasshopper imitations out of foam strips and rubber legs, with or without hair and feathers. There is no doubt these grasshopper flies catch fish, float all day long, and are more durable than hair and feather. But recently, on a number of western rivers, I've seen guides watch fish refuse foam hoppers a half-dozen times, pause, pull the boat over to the bank, and say, "Let's try a Dave's instead of that foam one." When it comes to fussy fish who have seen hundreds of imitation hoppers in a season, foam cut with scissors and glued on a hook might not give the same lifelike effect as feathers and hair, with their more subtle shape and movement.

Dave's Hopper is not an easy fly to tie, but once you master the various steps, you'll find it a most satisfying fly to have in your box. Although most of us don't have the artistic sensitivity of Dave Whitlock, we can all appreciate when a combination of feathers, hair, and yarn come together in a fly that not only looks terrific, but also catches fish when other hoppers won't.

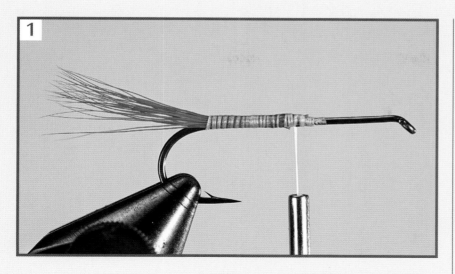

1 ■ Begin the yellow tying thread one-third of the way back from the eye of the hook. Bring the thread back to the part where the bend begins. Stack a sparse bunch of red deer hair and tie it in short, about half of the shank length. Begin with loose turns of thread so the tail does not flare too much, and as you advance the thread toward the eye, bind it down tighter. Trim the tail just short of where the thread began.

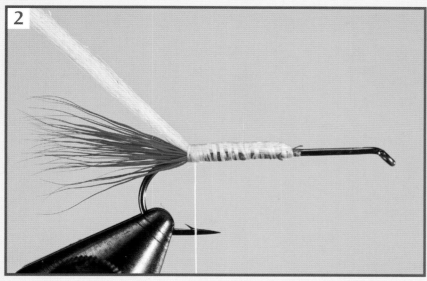

2 ■ For all but the largest flies, separate a piece of yellow polypropylene yarn into two strands. Snip one end of the yarn to even the ends and tie it in where the red deer hair ended. Wind over the yarn back to the tail.

3 ■ Loop the yarn over the tail so it is slightly shorter than the tail. Bind in the yarn with four very tight turns of thread to keep the loop in place. Push the long end of the yarn out of the way or hold it in a material clip.

4 ■ Prepare a brown hackle by stroking all of the fibers so they stand at 90-degree angles to the stem and trim them fairly close to the stem, about three-quarters of the length of the hook gape (the vertical distance between the point of the hook and the shank). Any hackle will work, from a big neck hackle to a saddle hackle. Use a feather you would not tie dry flies with to prevent waste. Trim the hackle very close to the stem, about half a hook-shank length, right at the tip.

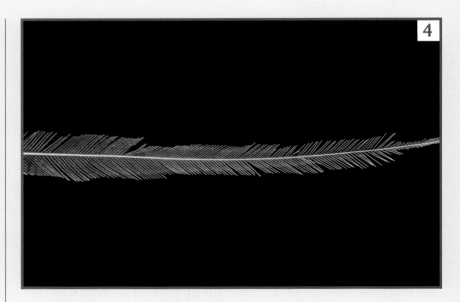

5 ■ Tie in the brown hackle by the tip and wind thread forward, binding the tip of the hackle under, until you get to the end point of the red deer hair and polypropylene yarn.

6 ■ Wind the polypropylene yarn forward in smooth turns. Tie it in where the ends of the other materials are, under the shank of the hook, to prevent too much bulk on top.

7 ■ Wind the trimmed hackle forward in even spirals. Tie it off under the hook shank as well. It's important to keep the forward third of the hook shank clean, as the deer-hair head will spin better on a bare hook.

8 ■ Cut and stack a sparse bunch of yellow deer hair. Tie it in over the top of the shank so it extends to the end of the looped yarn. Trim the ends very close to the hook. Head cement will be added to the body before the head is made, so keep the turns of thread to a minimum here.

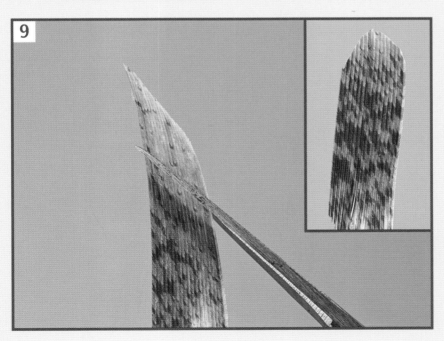

9 ■ From a stiffened turkey quill (see sidebar on page 19 for more information), separate a section of quill from adjacent fibers with your dubbing needle. The section should be slightly wider than the hook gape. If you look at the feather, you will notice that at one point the fibers begin to curve off to one side. Below that point, round the end of the feather section with one smooth cut, rotating the scissors around the feather as you cut to get a nice rounded shape.

10 ■ Bind the feather section to the top of the hook so that the edges curve around the sides a bit and the feather completely encloses the yellow bucktail. Trim the ends of the feather close to the hook shank.

11 ■ Prepare two legs by cutting six to eight fibers from a cock pheasant tail, making a loop in the section, and then pulling the tips of the feather through the loop with a pair of forceps or a crochet needle. If you find this difficult, wet the fibers before knotting them to help them stay together. (For an even easier solution, you can buy pheasant tail feathers with knots tied in the entire feather every six to eight fibers.) Trim about four fibers from the thicker "thigh" area to make the upper leg a little slimmer, and trim the ends of the fibers beyond the knot to get a better defined claw.

12 ■ Tie a leg to each side of the hook at the same place you tied in the wing. Tie them in one at a time, pulling the thread straight toward you to place the leg on the far side and straight away from you to attach the leg to the near side. The legs should angle upward just a bit and should extend to the end of the tail.

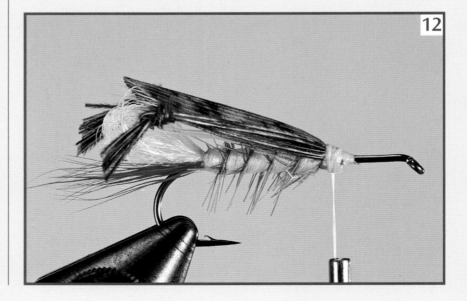

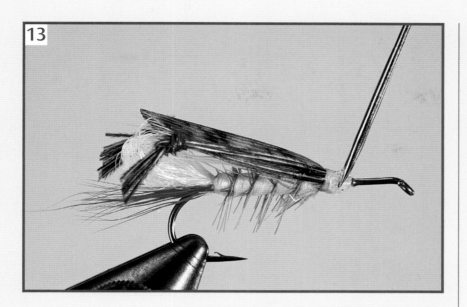

13 ▪ Bind in the wing and leg assemblies with four or five tight turns of thread, holding onto the legs and wing so they do not roll around the shank. Whip finish and apply head cement to the point where the legs and wing were tied in. At this point, if you are tying more than one Dave's Hopper, put the body/wing/leg assembly aside to dry and make duplicates.

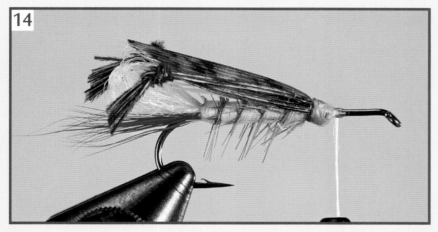

14 ▪ Attach the gray 3/0 thread on top of the wing and leg tie-in point. Advance it forward to a point where the shank is bare or almost bare.

15 ▪ Cut a bunch of hair from a piece of clean, coarse deer hair with straight fibers. The bunch should be about one-and-a-half times the hook gape in diameter. Clean all the fuzz and short hairs from the bunch by holding the tips and pulling on the butt ends. Then, bat the butt ends back and forth with your finger to expose any fuzz inside the bunch and pull it loose. Lay the bunch of deer hair over the wing, with the tips pointing backward. It should extend about halfway back on the wing. Take one loose turn over the hair. Take a second turn while allowing some of the fibers to slip from your fingers. Then, let go of the hair and make about four more very tight turns of thread, allowing the hair to flare all the way around the hook.

16 ▪ While still keeping tension on the thread, distribute the hair evenly 360 degrees around the hook by moving it around with the fingers of your other hand. With the nails of your thumb and forefinger, pinch the hook shank and push back at the winds at the base of the hair, compressing it as much as possible. Take two more tight turns of thread to lock the hair in place.

17 ▪ Cut another bunch of hair of the same size, but trim off the tips to make it easier to separate the hair that should be trimmed to form the head from the hair for the collar, which imitates the front legs of the hopper. Clean all the fuzz and short hairs from this bunch and tie it in the same way that you tied the first bunch. Make sure you compress this bunch in the same manner.

18 ▪ Whip finish, pushing any hairs out of the way as you do so to avoid binding them under. Take a new double-edged razor blade and either snap it in half carefully with two pairs of pliers or hold the blade in a small clamp. Double-edged safety razor blades are not sharp enough and won't work. You can trim the head either by holding the fly in your hand or by keeping it in a vise, with the eye of the fly pointing toward you. Start with the bottom of the head, and trim with a smooth sawing motion with the razor blade. Trim the fly carefully underneath as close to the shank as possible without cutting into the thread. Trim the hairs all the way back, including the tips of the collar hairs.

19 ■ Trim both sides of the hair in the same way, but avoid cutting all the way back; leave the fine tips of the collar hairs in place. Trim the top of the head in the same way. The finished head should be rectangular and slightly wider than it is tall, the same basic shape as a natural grasshopper.

20 ■ With a pair of small, sharp scissors, trim any of the blunt hairs that lay up against the collar.

21 ■ Apply deep-penetrating head cement (or cement thinned down so that it flows well) to the bare thread winds at the head. It helps to hold the fly nose-up to ensure that the thinned head cement flows back into the base of the hair and the thread winds that hold it.

Fly tiers have been creating imitations of caddis flies for 100 years because they rival mayflies as the most important food source for trout in running water. In fact, in some rivers, caddis flies far outnumber mayflies in abundance, both on the streambed and in the stomachs of trout. Early imitations of caddis flies used feathers, which didn't really present the tent-shaped caddis wing in a realistic profile. Around the middle of the 20th century, flies that used deer hair for the wings, like the Bucktail Caddis, became popular. They were far more durable than flies tied with feather wings and they floated better.

Al Troth was a pragmatic fly tier and fisherman from Pennsylvania who often fished the rivers of Montana during the summer. One year, he found an elk side on a ranch near Gallatin Gateway. The hide had been sitting outside for months and the skin was hard and stiff. Troth, convinced he had found a better material for wings on caddis flies, punched a hole in the hide and left it in a stream for three days to soften it up (and make sure all the critters vacated the hide). Back in Pennsylvania, he tied some flies he thought would be wet flies to imitate drowned and emerging caddis flies, but when he tried the first one on Loyalsock Creek, it kept popping to the surface due to the buoyant nature of the hollow elk hairs. A new dry fly was born, one

■ Al Troth

that works so well it is now in nearly every fly box in the world.

Troth believed in flies that were durable, easy to tie quickly, and effective. After tinkering with various types of elk hair, he settled on hair from the hide of a mature bull, which was stiffer (so it did not flare too much, just enough to get a caddis-like shape) and light-toned (so it was easy to see on

Hare's Ear Fur

Hare's ear fur is, of course, the essential ingredient to the deadly Hare's Ear nymph, but it is also just as valuable when tying dry flies. When incorporated into a nymph, the many spiky hairs of varying shades probably give the impression of movement, and the mixed look of the hairs is a more accurate representation of the body of an insect larva, which is seldom a monochromatic tone, but instead a mixture of many different shades. The same advantages make hare's ear excellent for dry flies, with the added advantage that the many tiny hairs help hold air bubbles and act like miniature hackle fibers in keeping the fly suspended in the surface film.

There is no commercial blend that gives you the same effect of the hare's ear fur that you make yourself. I've spent years trying to get commercial suppliers of packaged dubbing to make real hare's

By using the short, speckled hairs from the ears of a hare's mask combined with the softer fur of the face, you'll get a blend that offers spiky dubbing with mixed colors.

ear dubbing, but they always end up using plain rabbit fur with a few guard hairs mixed in, which just does not have the same magical effect of true hare's ear. It's apparently not cost-effective to pay people to sit around carefully cutting all the hair out of a pair of tiny ears when you can shave the whole hide of a rabbit in seconds.

Making hare's ear fur is not fun or easy, so I make large quantities of it every couple of years and package it for use. You can do this with a minimum of fuss and mess. Buy anywhere from one to a dozen hare's ears, depending on how much dubbing you want to make. (Before you feel sorry for these cute little furry creatures, you should know that these are ears from the European hares that were introduced into Australia and are considered a major invasive pest, causing millions of dollars in crop damage each year.)

Cut equal amounts of soft fur from the face of the rabbit, including the large guard hairs and the small dark hairs from the ears. When you trim the ears, make sure that you cut right down to the base of the ear because the hairs are quite short. To make a dark shade of hare's ear fur, use more of the black hairs from the ears and less from the soft fur on the face. To make a lighter shade, use more of the soft fur from the face. I like the darker variety, which has more spiky hairs and is buggier. Put all the fur you've cut in a bowl of water. Add a small amount of dish soap to help wet the fur. Swirl the hair and water mixture around until it is well mixed, then rinse all the soap off by dumping the fur in a fine-mesh colander and rinsing with plenty of water. Then, dump the soggy mess of hair on some newspaper and leave it to dry where it won't be disturbed by wind, pets, small children, or curious spouses. When the hair is completely dry, put it in a Ziploc bag and you'll have enough beautifully mixed hare's ear dubbing for many dozens of flies.

Pattern Description

Hook
Standard dry fly, sizes 10–18

Thread
Tan 6/0

Rib
Fine gold wire

Body
Hare's ear dubbing

Wing
Bleached bull elk

Hackle
Brown saddle or neck hackle

the water). Deer hair is darker in tone and harder to see in low light, and because it flares too much, it was tough for Troth to get it to hold the shape he wanted. He added a body of hare's ear fur, one of the best-floating furs, and a palmered hackle to help the fly float and to imitate the struggling legs of an adult caddis fly. He ribbed the palmered hackle with silver wire to make sure the delicate hackle stem would hold up to mouthing by dozens of trout before the fly fell apart. He later used bleached elk hair to get an even lighter color.

The pattern shown in this chapter is the original dressing as tied by Al Troth. He varied the body color to match the naturals, but honestly, the body is obscured by the hackle, which imitates the skittering legs of an adult caddis, and if you make the wing any darker it will not be as easy to see on the water. I seldom use any color but the original, which also makes a perfect moth imitation, as moths are an underestimated but important trout food.

Many Elk Hair Caddis flies you see today have large heads formed by the butts of the hair. Troth did not make his heads as big as most of the ones you see today. He did let some of the butt ends of the hair extend beyond the thread wraps, but just long enough to ensure that they didn't pull back through the winds. He applied liberal amounts of head cement to the ends of the hairs for this reason.

Troth also sometimes left the hackle off his Elk Hair Caddis imitations, especially for flat water, so the fly would have a cleaner profile. However, I've found that without hackle, the fly lands quite hard; I prefer a variation developed by Craig Matthews, the X-Caddis. The X-Caddis uses a wing of deer instead of elk, and a trailing shuck made of Z-Lon yarn. It is more like an imitation of an emerging caddis than an adult skittering across the surface. It seems to be better than the Elk Hair Caddis in flat water because it lands lighter due to its bulkier deer-hair wing, and also because fish in flat water are more likely to be taking an emerger than a skittering adult.

Pattern Variation

X-CADDIS

Hook: Standard dry fly, sizes 10–18

Thread: Match body color, 6/0

Trailing Shuck: Z-Lon yarn, to match body color, tied as a heavy tail

Body: Superfine dubbing, to match natural
- Common colors are olive, bright green, tan, brown, gray, and cream.

Wing: Fine deer hair without long black tips (often sold as Sparkle Dun hair or Comparadun hair)

1 ▪ Start the thread about one third of the way back from the eye of the hook. Wind the thread in a single layer back to the beginning of the bend of the hook. Catch a four-inch piece of gold wire under the thread. The wire should extend about three-quarters of the way down the hook shank.

2 ▪ Wind the thread forward over the wire with smooth, tight wraps. Once you pass the end of the wire, continue the thread to just behind the eye and then wind back to a point one-quarter of the hook-shank length back from the eye.

3 ▪ Prepare a brown hackle with fibers that are just barely longer than the gape of the hook by stroking the fibers at the bottom of the feather back so they lie at right angles to the stem. Cut the webby butt end of the hackle off and trim the fibers very close to either side of the stem about half a hook-shank length.

4 ▪ Tie in the hackle feather, the tip pointing out over the eye and the trimmed butt lying on top of the shank. Bind it in with smooth, even turns, working back toward the bend. Leave a small piece of trimmed stubs showing so that when you begin winding the hackle you have a little part to work with in case you need to manipulate it a bit to make it lie in place properly. The little nubs of hackle that you bind under will keep the hackle stem from pulling out no matter how hard you yank on it when you wind it.

5 ▪ When the thread is all the way back to the wire tie-in point, wax the thread thoroughly with very sticky wax. Dub about three to four inches of the thread with

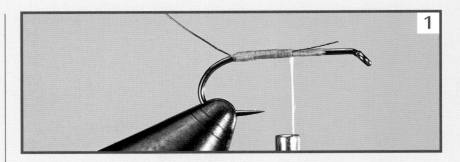

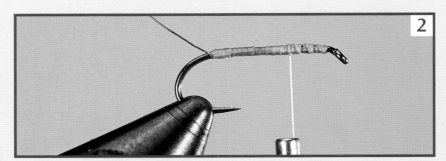

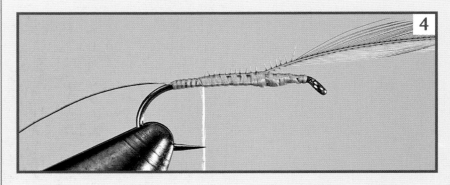

hare's ear fur, starting with a tiny amount of dubbing at the top of the thread and gradually increasing the diameter of fur you add. Then, make a slight taper at the bottom. The body should be substantial, not sparse. Aim for a smooth taper when you dub, and fuss with the fur a bit until you have no lumps or thin spots in your dubbing. It's easier to fix any problems before you begin dubbing.

6 ▪ Wind the dubbing forward to cover about three-quarters of the hook shank. If you end up with too long a section of dubbing, back up, pick some off, and then bear down on the new end so that it does not get sloppy at the end. If you don't have enough to finish, unwind a few turns and dub a small amount farther down on the thread.

7 ▪ Leave the thread hanging in place. Grab the hackle and wind it back toward the bend with even, open spirals. The hackle should slant back slightly to the rear as you wind it. It will usually take four to six turns of hackle, depending on the feather and the size hook you have chosen.

8 ▪ When you get to a point just shy of the end of the body, hold the hackle pliers above the hook and switch hands. Grab the piece of wire and make one turn right at the end of the body, then catch the hackle with the wire to bind it under. Wind the wire back through the hackle with the same number of evenly spaced turns as you used to wind the hackle. Change the angle of the wire slightly and wiggle it back and forth as you wind to prevent binding under too many hackle fibers. When you get beyond the last turn of hackle, secure the wire with several tight turns of tying thread.

9 ■ Snip the end of the hackle as close to the body as possible.

10 ■ Snip a bunch of elk hair from a hide. The exact amount will depend on the size you are tying and how full you want your fly to look. The fuller the wing, the better it floats and the easier it is to see, but if the wing is too full, it won't cinch down properly and will twist around the hook. Remove the fuzz and short hairs at the base of the bunch by holding the hair at the tips and pulling firmly with your thumb and forefinger at the butt ends of the hairs. Place the hair in a stacker and rap firmly a few times. I also like to twirl the hair a few times in between raps with the stacker to mix up the hairs and remove any bias the bunch might have to cock to one side or the other. Twirling the hairs mixes them up so that the curvature of any piece of hair is negated by the one next to it. Remove the end of the stacker and grab the tips of the hairs firmly with your thumb and forefinger, clamping down on the bunch so the ends stay even.

11 ■ Measure the hair bunch against the fly. The wing should not extend past the bend of the hook. (Troth realized that real caddis wings extend past the end of the body, but found that this fly just fished better if the wing was not longer than the body.)

12 ■ Hold the hair over the hook shank where you want it with your right thumb and forefinger and then grasp the wing with the ends of your left thumb and forefinger immediately over the tie-in point. Pinch the hair against the hook and make a firm turn of thread over the hair. Unlike deer hair, elk will not flare

very much, nor does it tend to roll over the side of the hook as readily. Take seven or eight very tight turns over the hair, tightening with a downward pull on the thread while keeping it pinched against the top and sides of the hook. Move just slightly forward and increase the tension with each turn.

13 ■ Lift the butt ends of the hair up, take a few turns of thread under the wing, and whip finish. To keep from whipping any of the butt ends of thread under, you can cradle the bobbin in the palm of your left hand while using the thumb and forefinger of the same hand to pull the hairs up out of the way as you whip finish with your right hand. Many tiers don't take this extra step and just whip finish on top of the wing windings. I find that taking a few winds under the wing and cocking the butt ends of the wings up slightly helps keep it from rolling around the shank of the hook after some use, and gives the fibers of the wing added security against pulling out.

14 ■ Hold the butt ends of the hair up at a 45-degree angle from the hook shank. Put a pair of sharp scissors at the same angle and snip the ends of the hair almost flush to the hook shank, leaving short nubs of hair to form the head of the fly. Many tiers today leave a much larger head than this, but Troth always trimmed his heads fairly close.

15 ■ This fly deserves two applications of head cement: one on the entire circumference of the bare thread winds that hold the wing in place, and one on the butt ends of the hair. Make sure you use deep-penetrating or thinned head cement for this fly so the cement seeps into the ends of the wing.

3 Griffith's Gnat

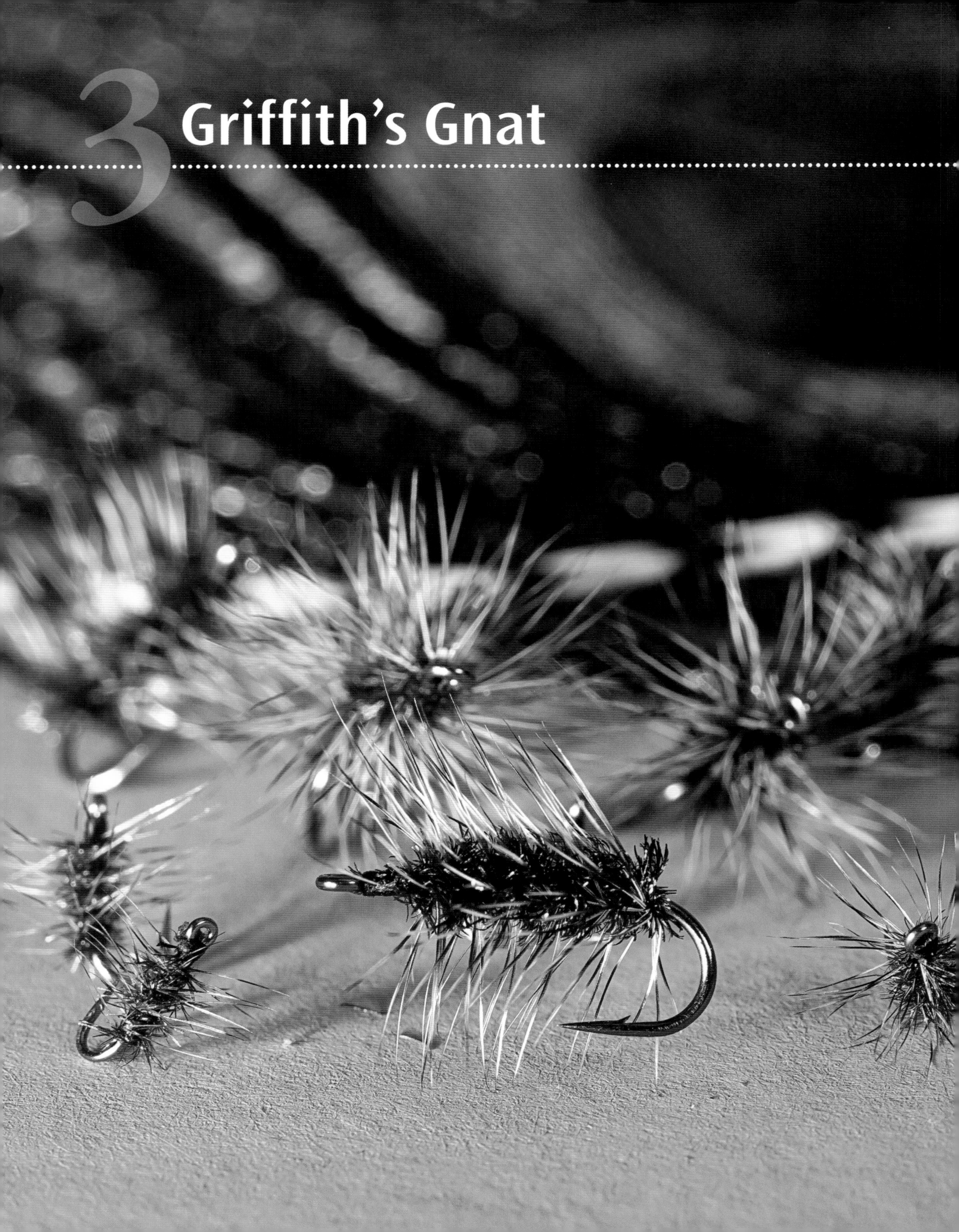

Trout Unlimited officially began with a gathering of 16 people in the living room of George Griffith's lodge, The Barbless Hook, on Michigan's Ausable River. It was July 1959, and although 40 people were invited, it was midsummer and many were vacationing with their families. It was not a chance meeting, and the groundwork had been laid for almost 20 years.

Fishermen throughout Michigan had been worried for decades about a number of issues that threatened to destroy wild trout fishing. Paramount was unchecked pollution and habitat degradation, but almost as important was the entrenched position of a fish culture cabal with Michigan politicians. When anglers complained about a lack of fish in a trout stream, the state would promptly dispatch a train filled with fat, stupid trout that would either be caught in a matter of weeks or perish. Although the original intent of Trout Unlimited (TU) was to form a small but elite group of anglers to influence fisheries policy in Michigan only, once the word got out, the concept took on a life of its own. Conservation-minded trout fishermen, sick of antiquated state policies that relied on fish culture and hearsay instead of science, couldn't wait to organize.

Griffith served as president of Trout Unlimited from 1961 to 1964, and remained active in TU for the rest of his

■ George Griffith

Hook
Standard or Bigeye dry fly, sizes 14–24

Thread
Black 10/0

Tail
Tying thread

Rib
Tying thread

Body
Thin peacock herl

Hackle
Grizzly, palmered through body

long life. He had the pleasure of seeing it grow from 855 members and revenue of $15,000 in its first year to a membership of more than 150,000 members with revenue of about $12 million. Over the course of Griffith's lifetime, Trout Unlimited made active trout conservationists of more than a quarter-million anglers.

It's a common misconception that George Griffith developed the fly we know as the Griffith's Gnat. He didn't. No one knows who developed the Griffith's Gnat; that part of the story I could not decipher even after writing a biography of him and reading his autobiography. It was apparently first tied by one of his fishing buddies and named after the great conservationist. But not only was the fly not developed by George Griffith, it's not likely a pattern he often used.

When trout sip tiny unknown insects from the surface film, it's a perfect time to tie on a Griffith's Gnat.

Tying with Peacock Herl

Most tiers, when a pattern calls for peacock herl, just grab a few fibers from a loose bag of herl. However, you should spend almost as much effort obtaining the right size herl as you do choosing hackle. This is difficult when you buy loose bags of peacock herl, so always buy whole eyed feathers. Only with an entire feather can you select herls with different flue lengths (the flues are the tiny fibers on the side of each herl that gives the feather its iridescent sheen). In fact, it's best to buy peacock eyed tail feathers in multiples, because each tail feather differs in length depending on its position in the tail. By having three or four different feathers on your tying desk, you can always find the right size. From a single feather, here's a guide to picking the right herls:

- For flies sizes 8 to 12, select five herls from just below the eyed portion of the tail feather. This is the place where the flues are densest and longest.

- For flies sizes 14 to 18, select four herls from the bottom of a large tail feather or from a small eye.

- For size 18 and smaller flies, select two herls from a small peacock eye or from the top of a large eye.

When tying with peacock herl, always tie in the herls by their tips. Peacock herl flues have a distinct curve to them, which should face backward when winding the herl; otherwise, the flues bind themselves under and the fly looks scraggly and sparse. By tying in by the tips, the flues will almost naturally sweep backward when you begin winding. If you notice they are not facing in the right direction, back off a turn and try to align the fibers properly by twisting the herls a half turn.

Peacock herls are fragile and often break during casting or when cut by fish teeth. There are a number of ways to strengthen them. One way is to twist the herls together before winding, which makes a stronger body but does not look quite as buggy. Alternatively, herls can be twisted in a loop of tying thread with the same process used to make a dubbing loop. Many tiers use a rib of fine wire to reinforce the herls as well. When tying small Griffith's Gnats, I don't like the extra weight added by using wire, so I rib the fly with tying thread.

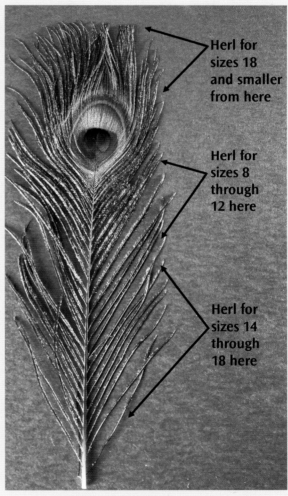

Herl for sizes 18 and smaller from here

Herl for sizes 8 through 12 here

Herl for sizes 14 through 18 here

■ Not all peacock herl is the same. The smallest fibers are at the very top above the eye, the largest are found along the bottom sides of the eye, and the intermediate-sized fibers are at the bottom. In addition, smaller eyes than this nice full one may have smaller herls in the same spots on the feather.

Pattern Variation

HI-VIS GRIFFITH'S GNAT

Hook: Standard or Bigeye dry fly, sizes 14–24

Thread: Black 10/0

Rib: Tying thread

Body: Thin peacock herl

Post: Red, orange, white, or chartreuse Para-Post or similar high-visibility yarn

Hackle: Grizzly, palmered through body

Note: It's hard to improve on a fly as effective as the Griffith's Gnat and most anglers use the original version. However, it floats so low in the water that it is sometimes difficult to spot. In that case, tie a post of bright yarn in the middle of the body before winding the peacock herl and hackle.

George Griffith was first and foremost a streamer fisherman and was not interested in matching the hatch. He had no time for small flies or small fish, and often told his fishing buddy, rod builder Bob Summers, that "a big fish is not going to exert all that energy for something that's going to get stuck between its teeth." But although he didn't spend much time worrying about hatches, he was very much a scientist in his fishing. He knew where every big fish would be, and how all the big logjams in the water ended up where they were. He was superb at reading the water, believing the most important part of fly fishing was getting the fly to where the trout lived. He spent little time worrying about fly patterns, but was constantly fussing with his leader to get it just right.

There is another reason that Griffith would not have developed a midge imitation. Although Griffith tied flies, there was a long gap in his fly-tying career. He lost his right eye while fishing a big streamer in the rain, removing his glasses to wipe them just as the streamer hit his face. But 30 years later, a doctor looked at his eye and thought he could remove the scar tissue, and after an operation his sight was restored and he began tying again. Most of his flies, however, were big, meaty streamers.

Nevertheless, it's fitting that we honor this legendary conservationist with one of the best trout flies ever designed. Most anglers consider the fly an imitation of clumper midges, which is an angler's description for a situation where groups of adult midges—when forming mating swarms above and on the surface of the water—form groups of anywhere from two to a half-dozen midges that cling to each other while floating in the current. Trout often feed selectively on these clumps, ignoring single midges that float by. In this case, even though the fly is a midge imitation, it is effective as large as a size 14.

The utility of this fly goes far beyond an imitation of a clumper midge. In smaller sizes, it is an excellent imitation of a single midge pupa at the moment of emergence. And the reason it works so well whenever trout rise to small flies is because it imitates many other terrestrial *Diptera* that fall into the water—tiny beetles, leafhoppers, and other small terrestrial bugs—of which there are thousands in a single square foot of vegetation on the banks of a river. So don't relegate this fly just to times when you see midges on the water. It's a go-to fly for many experienced anglers whenever they suspect trout are feeding on tiny flies but can't figure out exactly what the fish are eating.

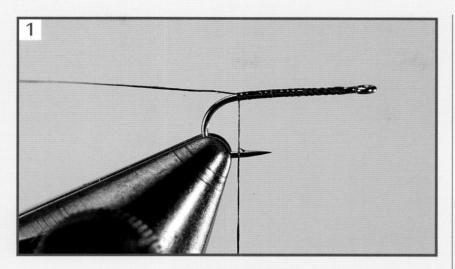

1 ■ Start the thread up close to the eye, but leave a long tag end and continue winding over it to the point over the barb. Pull this long thread out of the way and hang it on top of the vise stem or place it in a material clip.

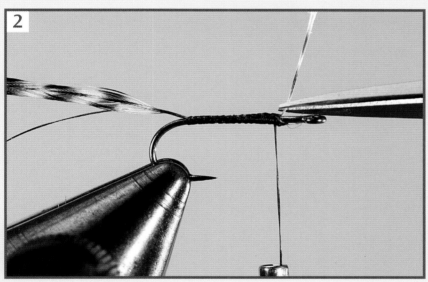

2 ■ Select a grizzly hackle with fibers that are just slightly longer than the hook gape. The hackle on this fly should not be too long. Strip the fibers from the base of the feather and tie it in, leaving a fairly long area of bare stem showing. Wind over the stem to about seven-eighths of the way to the eye. Snip off any remaining hackle stem close to the shank of the hook.

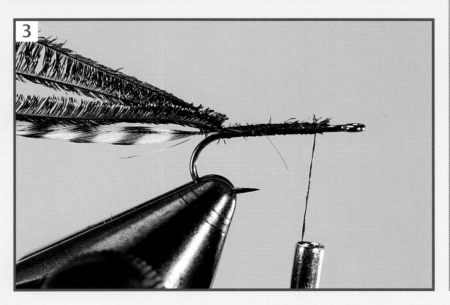

3 ■ Select some peacock herl with short flues for the body. Even the tips of the peacock herls to make them easier to tie in. Bind them under, working toward the bend and stopping where the hackle feather was first tied in.

4 ■ Wind the peacock herl forward to just behind the eye. Tie off four turns of tight thread.

5 ■ Wind the grizzly forward in even spirals. It should be quite dense, with closely spaced turns. Tie off the hackle just ahead of where the body ends with a half-dozen tight turns of thread.

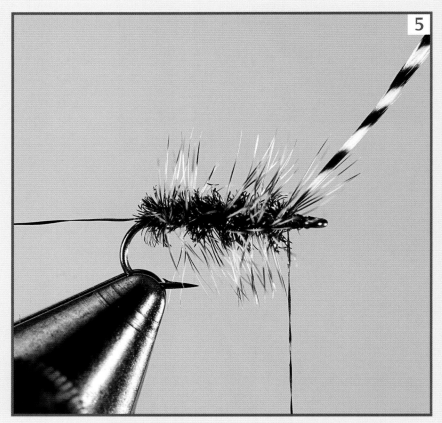

6 ■ Counterwrap the body and hackle with the thread that was left hanging. It won't bind any hackle fibers under if you weave it through carefully, and it adds durability to the body and hackle.

7 ■ Take another few wraps at the head, whip finish, and add a drop of deep-penetrating head cement to the bare thread wraps at the head.

4 Parachute Adams

As of this writing, the Parachute Adams is the most popular fly in the world, based on the sales of the two largest fly distributors. This is not likely to change anytime soon. It could be argued that the Woolly Bugger is used more often, and because it catches a wider variety of fish, it is responsible for more fly-caught fish than any other fly. But since the Woolly Bugger is such an easy fly to create, many anglers tie their own; thus, many of the Buggers used don't make it into sales figures. Besides, when you get down into the details, more fly anglers fish for trout than any other species; most people, when given the option, prefer fishing a floating fly; and the Parachute Adams is not an easy pattern to tie so that it looks neat and pretty (thus the reason for its overwhelming sales).

I can't even count the number of times I've seen the Parachute Adams on someone's "If I only had five trout flies to use for a season" list. It would certainly be on mine. During midge hatches on the Bighorn River, I've been out-fished by friends using size 18 or 20 Parachute Adams flies while I stuck to more precise and exacting midge imitations. I've had great success using big size 8 Parachute Adams flies with extended bodies during hatches of the giant *Hexagenia* mayfly. For no apparent reason, the Parachute Adams catches fish during caddis hatches, even though it does not look anything like a caddis fly. It seems to be effective when trout are eating terrestrial insects or mayflies that don't have a touch of gray or brown in them. The Parachute Adams is just one of those mystical flies with the right combination of materials

Pattern Description

to appeal to trout. It's not wise to question this too deeply.

Fifteen years ago, the standard Adams, with upright and divided wings and conventional hackle, would have beaten the Parachute Adams in a Top 10 Flies list. Why did the parachute version pull way ahead of its more traditional cousin? Most fly fishers pull the Parachute Adams out of their fly boxes before the traditional version because it is far easier to see on the water. Visibility has always been important with dry flies, not only because you can see the fly being inhaled, but also to help avoid drag. If you can't see the fly, you don't know if it's in the right place, drifting without the influence of the leader and line pulling on it, and many casts are wasted. The growth in popularity of fishing "dry dropper"—with a nymph hung below a highly visible dry—has made the Parachute Adams a go-to fly, as the standard version just doesn't cut it for either visibility or flotation.

There may be another reason for the popularity of the Parachute Adams as well. We now realize that trout prefer an emerging insect trapped in the surface film to one that has already escaped the meniscus, fluttering on the surface and free to fly away any second. Parachute flies by nature keep the body and tails of the fly right in the surface film, whereas a high-floating traditional fly often rides on its tiptoes, with only the points of the hackle and the tails touching the water.

The Parachute Adams is a variation of the aforementioned traditional Adams dry fly, an old pattern as dry flies go. The original Adams was first tied in 1922 for the Boardman River in Michigan by an experienced angler and fly tier named Leonard Halliday. An angler from Lorain, Ohio, Charles F. Adams, was fishing the fly in a small pond in front of Halliday's house and had planned to fish the evening hatch on the Boardman that evening. Halliday handed Adams a new pattern he had just created. "When he came back the next morning," Halliday reported, "he wanted know what I called it. He said it was a 'knock-out' and I said we would call it the Adams, since he had made the first good catch on it."

In the first half of the 20th century the dissemination of new fly patterns was not instantaneous as it is today; even good books on fly fishing and fly tying were typically printed in very small print runs and almost impossible to obtain. But by mid-century the Adams was a popular and effective dry fly. It had survived the crucible of many years of fishing and was carried forward more as oral history than in any kind of written media. The original Adams mutated slightly as it evolved. Halliday's original pattern called for a body of gray wool, which was replaced by gray fur, usually from a water animal since their fur is naturally water-repellent. When I first tied Adams flies commercially in the early 1970s, the only acceptable material was muskrat fur—due to its hydrophobic nature and lifelike silvery sheen—and I still use muskrat fur off a hide today as opposed to commercially blended dubbings.

Halliday's original pattern also called for "two strands from a golden pheasant neck feather." Over the years this has been misrepresented by angling historians as golden pheasant tippet fibers, but while examining an Adams tied by Halliday in the collection at the American Museum of Fly Fishing, I realized he used not the black-tipped orange tippet feathers from the upper neck, but the feathers just below the tippets, which are a uniform reddish-brown shade. And despite what Halliday wrote, he sometimes used more than two fibers, because the sample I examined used at least a dozen. No one knows who first replaced the golden pheasant fibers with mixed brown and grizzly hackle fibers, but that version is how we recognize the Adams today.

At about the same time the Adams was finding its way into fly boxes across North America, a young fly tier in Scotland, Helen Todd, invented the parachute fly in 1931. Her original pattern used pig's bristles for the parachute post, and the firm she tied for, Alex Martin, patented the design and began selling parachute flies almost exclusively. Alex Martin designed special hooks with a wire post incorporated into the design, and a similar hook was patented by William Brush of Detroit in 1934. Unfortunately, the added weight on top of the hook shank caused by the wire post made these flies poor floaters, perhaps one reason why they faded into obscurity for a number of years. They never went away completely, though. Herters sold a similar parachute hook for many years, and parachute flies still appeared in the English Veniard's fly catalog throughout the 20th century. But it was not until the 1970s—with the publication of Doug Swisher and Carl Richards's groundbreaking hatch-matching book *Selective Trout*—that parachute flies graduated to mainstream fly collections. Along with their more popular no-hackle flies, Swisher and Richards also

Pattern Variations

TRADITIONAL ADAMS

Hook: Standard dry fly, sizes 10–20

Thread: Black 6/0 or 8/0

Tail: Mixed brown and grizzly spade hackle fibers

Body: Natural muskrat fur, or any medium gray fur

Wing: Pair of grizzly hackle tips from a wide rooster or hen hackle

- Usually tied in a standard upright position divided at about a 30-degree angle, although sometimes tied (as the original was) semi-spent with the wings about 45 degrees apart.

Hackle: Brown and grizzly mixed, neck or saddle hackle

PARACHUTE HARE'S EAR
(Developed by Ed Schroeder)

Hook: Standard dry fly, sizes 10–20

Thread: Black 6/0 or 8/0

Tail: Deer hair, dark, short, and bulky

Body: Natural hare's ear fur, tied rough and heavy

Wing: Large bunch of white calf tail or calf body hair

Hackle: Grizzly, tied parachute-style and very heavy

Mixing Hackles

As if tying a parachute fly was not difficult enough, the Parachute Adams adds the complexity of mixing hackles from two different colored capes. In most dry flies, when using hackles of the same color, if two hackles are needed the best way to ensure that the hackle fibers match up in length is to pick both hackles from the same place on a cape or saddle. If both hackles have fibers of the same length, the fly looks neater and more conventional. Does it matter? Perhaps not. Uniform hackle fibers are supposed to make a dry fly float better and that's why it is convention for the uniform-hackle look, but I'm not really sure. Regardless, I take pains to make my hackles line up properly and most tiers feel the same. For commercially tied flies that must sell in the case of a fly shop, the way the hackle looks is a sign of a quality fly.

When taking feathers from two different capes the problem is magnified. Each chicken is unique and there is no guarantee that hackles taken from about the same place on each cape will have hackle fibers of the same length. In order to mix one grizzly and one brown hackle, the feathers should be measured against

the hook or a hackle gauge for the correct size. Also, as there is some leeway on what the correct hackle size should be (anywhere from one-and-a-half to two times the gape of the hook), two feathers that are appropriate for a size 14 fly might not look uniform once tied in. One way of getting around this issue is to use feathers from a rare (and thus expensive) color of hackle called cree, which combines brown, black, and white barring. But expense aside, a cree hackle never has the same strongly barred look as when grizzly and brown are mixed, and the hallmark of the Adams's effectiveness is strongly mixed colors that may simulate the tiny movements of a live insect.

There is some trial-and-error involved. The best approach is to pluck feathers from each neck that appear to have fibers of the same length and then flare them together to see how they look. One way of doing this is to flare both feathers together around the hook, which gives both the assurance that the feathers have an appropriate fiber length for the hook and that they have almost exactly the same length. Another way to check is to stroke the fibers at the bottom of both fe-

Left: The matched brown and grizzly hackles on the left won't look neat in a finished fly; although they are both appropriate for a size 14 hook, the brown fibers are shorter than the grizzly fibers. The two feathers on the right are much closer in length and will tie a better-looking fly. **Right:** The brown neck hackle on the left is from the middle of the stem and won't have the long, stiff fibers needed for dry-fly tails. The spade hackle on the right, from the side of the cape, gives better tail fibers.

■ Lay both colors of tailing fibers on the edge of a table or vise pedestal, then carefully pick them up with your fingertips.

athers until they stand at right angles to the stem, laying them down one on top of the other to see how closely they line up. If they don't line up, place one of the feathers in a small box or Ziploc bag for use later with a matching feather from the other color.

Mixing the tails on an Adams is even harder and absolutely frivolous. I am certain you could use just brown or just grizzly for the tails and never get a refusal from a trout. But that's the way the pattern is tied, and if you want to recreate this killer in its proper form—so that when you show off the flies in your box to a friend on the river you can beam when he or she admires your talent—get used to mixing the tails. I like to lay one bunch on the edge of my pedestal vise with the tips sticking over the edge so it's easy to lay the other half of the fibers on top of them with the ends lined up. Then I can carefully pick up the bunch all together. Try to pick them up with your fingers without changing their alignment, or pick them up by moistening a fingertip and placing it straight down on top of them. Put the fibers in a thin stacker if you wish to make them look perfectly aligned.

Tails should come from spade feathers from the side of a neck hackle cape. These are short, wide triangular feathers that are not of much use for dry-fly hackles but are perfect for tails. The fibers on these feathers are stiffer and longer than any other feather on a cape, and even if you tie all of your dry flies with saddle hackles instead of neck hackles, it's wise to have at least one neck cape just for tails. Saddle hackles seldom have fibers that are long or stiff enough. Many fly-tying companies used to sell really stiff, glossy spade hackles by themselves in small packs, but that practice seems to have gone out of style, perhaps because many tiers substitute either hairs like moose or synthetic nylon fibers for spade hackles. I find hair tails fine for bigger, bulkier flies, but they don't have the delicacy of spade hackles for smaller flies. And the synthetic nylon fibers, although they look fine, are more flexible than spade hackle fibers and tend to foul around the hook bend after repeated false casting.

developed the Paradun fly, which utilized both turkey body feathers and hair from moose and elk as post and wing.

It was a natural progression to try parachute flies not only for specific insect imitations, but also for more general attractor patterns like the Adams. I am not totally certain who first tied the Adams in a parachute version with a white hair wing, but it may have been a brilliant fly tier from Pennsylvania, Dave Kashner, who ran the fly department at Orvis for many years. The first instance in print of a Parachute Adams as we know of it today was in the 1967 Orvis catalog, where parachute versions of popular dry flies of the day like the Light Cahill and Black Gnat appeared. Whether Kashner developed these variants by himself or obtained them from someone else is not known, but all of the parachute flies smoldered for a few years— all except the Adams version, which gradually ignited and rose to the top of the dry-fly category.

1 ■ Attach thread to the center of the shank and wind back to the normal tail tie-in point. Pull about 15 fibers of brown spade hackle away from the center of the stem until their ends are even. Tweak them from the stem with a brisk pull to keep them aligned. Lay them down gently. Do the same thing with grizzly hackle fibers and lay the grizzly on top of the brown so they are lined up.

2 ■ Tie the tail fibers in by holding them at a slight angle to the shank, with the butt ends angled slightly toward the near side of the hook shank and the tail ends pointing slightly away from you. When you begin winding thread over them, the tails should align neatly on top of the hook shank. Wind forward to the middle of the hook shank. Trim the remaining butt ends of the fibers.

3 ■ Continue to wind the thread over the bare hook, stopping just shy of the eye and then winding back toward the bend, stopping at a point slightly forward of the point you would for tying a standard winged dry fly, or about one-fifth of the hook-shank length instead of one-quarter of the shank length back from the eye.

4 ■ Cut a bunch of white calf tail from the base of a tail with relatively straight hairs, or cut a bunch of calf body hair with fine, straight fibers. Before you clean and stack it, the bunch should be twice the diameter of the hook gape. Pinch the hair by the tips, about three-quarters of the way down from the tips, and pull all fuzz and short hairs from the base of the bunch. Place the hair in a stacker to even it up. Calf hair,

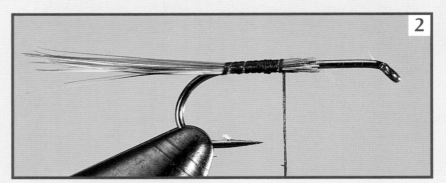

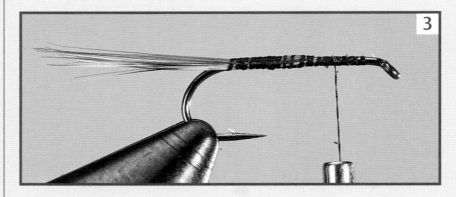

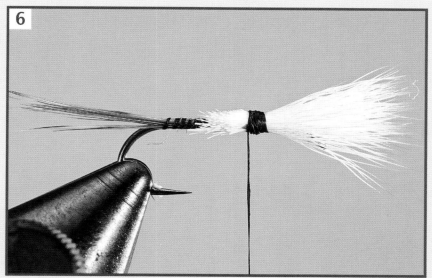

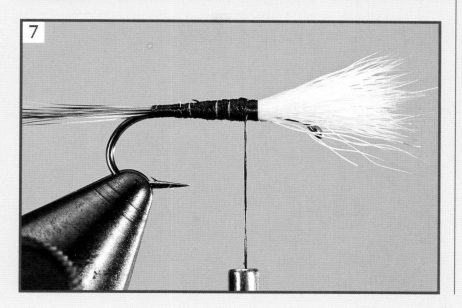

unlike elk hair, requires repeated short, staccato taps as opposed to the several sharp wraps you would use with coarser hair. If the hair still does not line up, remove it from the stacker, roll it around in your fingers, and stack a second time.

5 ■ Measure the calf hair against the shank. The wing should be equal to the length of the shank. Tie in the calf hair with a half-dozen very tight pinch wraps, allowing no letup in tension between each wrap. Each subsequent wrap should move slightly toward the tails, but should still overlap the turn before it. If the hair rolls to one side, back up a couple of turns, roll it back on top of the hook, and take a few more tight turns.

6 ■ Lift up the butt ends of the hair and trim them on a slight taper toward the rear. Unlike elk or deer hair, calf hair does not compress and thus you can't bury the butt ends under tight thread. You just have to deal with the bulk and cut it off at an angle, which is not easy when the hair wants to roll over the hook as you trim it. It's worth the effort to make a number of cuts with a pair of sharp, fine-pointed scissors, working from the far side to the top and then to the near side.

7 ■ Cover the ends of the hair with smooth wraps of thread, building up a nice tapered underbody.

8 ■ Bring the thread in front of the wing. Pinch the wing at its base and raise it straight up, then build a tight, slightly tapered dam of thread in front of the wing. Keep wrapping up against the front base of the wing until it stands upright on its own.

9 ■ Wind about six tight turns of thread around the base of the wing by bringing the bobbin tube close to the base of the wing and winding clockwise around its base, with the bobbin horizontal, while holding the wing upright with your fingers.

10 ■ Wind the thread back to the base of the tail. Dub a thin body of muskrat fur with the guard hairs removed on the thread. The body should be very thin close to the hook, fattening just slightly as you get closer to your bobbin. Since the body already has a taper, you don't want to compound the bulkiness of the front of the body, so the taper of this fur should be very slight.

11 ■ Wind the dubbing forward in even, slightly overlapping turns so the thread underneath does not show. When you get to the wing, make a tight figure eight around the base of the wing and end up in front of the wing with just a small amount of dubbing on the shank.

12 ■ Select a brown and a grizzly saddle or neck hackle with fibers that are one-and-a-half times the length of the hook gape. The exact length is not as important as the fact that their fibers are exactly the same length, or the distance from the stem to the tip of their fibers. This will make the fly look neater. Stroke the fibers at the base of the feathers at right angles to the hook and trim them very close to the stem for a short section at the base of the feather.

13 ■ Tie in both hackle butts together right in front of the wing with three tight turns of thread. It helps to keep the dull sides of the feathers facing up if possible. Don't trim the butts of the feathers yet.

14 ■ Stand the hackles up against the wing and wrap the thread up the base of the wing, trapping the trimmed stems of both hackles. Try to keep the dull sides of the feathers facing out. Wrap the thread back down the base of the wing and take two more tight turns over the wing butts. By tying in the hackles this way, they will never slip out as you tie them no matter how much pressure you put on them. Leave the thread hanging right in front of the wing.

15 ■ Grasp both hackles together and manipulate them so that the dull sides are facing down. This keeps the curvature of the hackles pointing down, which makes a neater fly. Once they are positioned properly, grab both hackles together and take one turn of hackle around the wing just above where the black thread winds left off. Take a second turn immediately below this turn, and then take a third turn of hackle under the second one. End up with the hackles over the shank, over the eye, just slightly to the far side.

16 ■ Trap the hackle fibers against the hook shank with your fingers while pulling back on the parachute hackle winds. Take three turns of thread, as tight as you can make them, over both hackle feathers just in front of the wing and just slightly to the far side of the top of the hook shank. While still holding the parachute hackle back out of the way with your fingers, bring the point of a sharp pair of fine-pointed scissors to where the hackles meet the hook shank and snip them as close to the hook as possible. Make several more tight turns of thread over the tie-off point.

17 ▦ Add just a tiny amount of muskrat fur to the thread and wind it over the point just in front of the wing, then dub forward almost to the eye. Remove a tiny bit of dubbing if you have too much or add just a bit of fuzz to the thread if you don't have quite enough. Make two more turns of bare thread up against the eye.

18 ▦ Whip finish and add a drop of head cement to the bare thread winds and to the top of the hackle winds at the base of the wing. Many people have trouble whip finishing parachute flies, but if you angle your whip finisher about 45 degrees to the horizontal you should be able to sneak your knot under the hackle without wrapping it. If you still have a problem, you can hold the hackle out of the way with your fingers while you whip finish.

19 ▦ Apply a drop of head cement to the bare thread winds at the eye and a second drop at the base of the wing where the hackle winds begin.

The line between eastern and western dry flies has been mostly eliminated over the past 20 years. Big foam flies and giant stone fly imitations are used regularly on eastern waters, and with increasing fish pressure on Rocky Mountain trout and the popularity of tailwaters and spring creeks in the West, smaller, sparser flies have become standard on waters where at one time all you needed was a size 12 Royal Wulff. Sparsely tied Catskill-style dry flies have a place in every angler's fly box, and although many of the legendary Catskill patterns are no longer sold in fly shops, one fly that remains a stalwart is Art Flick's Red Quill.

Although Flick tied this fly as an imitation of the male dun or subimago of the mayfly species *Ephemerella subvaria*, known to anglers as the Hendrickson, it has far more utility than Flick originally intended. It makes a very fine imitation of many spinners, especially when they first fall on the water with upright wings. (It's fascinating that Flick dismissed Hendricksons as not worth his time, perhaps because Catskill tiers seldom tied their flies with spent wings. I have fished amazing Hendrickson spinner falls on the very stream that Flick fished, the Schoharie in the northern Catskills.) And the Red Quill is also one of the best imitations for the Western March Brown mayfly, especially on windy days when the flies flutter across the surface of the water.

In 1947, Putnam published a little book on trout-stream insects and their imitations called *Art Flick's Streamside Guide*. To put it into per-

■ A Red Quill tied for the author by Art Flick in the 1980s. The long head, typical of Catskill flies, was to facilitate the once-popular Turle knot, which loops over the head of the fly.

Hook
Standard dry fly, sizes 12–16

Thread
Black 8/0 or 10/0

Tail
Dark blue dun hackle fibers, stiff

Body
Stripped and soaked quill from a Rhode Island Red rooster, or other natural dark brown hackle feather without a black center

Wing
Wood duck flank feather

Hackle
Dark blue dun

Pattern Variation

DUN VARIANT

Hook: Standard dry fly, sizes 12–16

Thread: Black 8/0 or 10/0

Tail: Dark blue dun hackle fibers, stiff and one-and-a-half times the hook-shank length

Body: Stripped and soaked quill from a Rhode Island Red rooster, or other natural dark brown hackle feather without a black center

Hackle: Dark blue dun, at least twice as long as the hook gape and occupying almost the entire forward one-third of the hook shank

spective, it was only the third book on American trout-stream insects to date. The first was Louis Rhead's 1916 book, *American Trout-Stream Insects.* Rhead's flies were wacky and well ahead of their time, and he ignored both the conventions of entomology and fly tying. Next, in 1935, came Preston Jennings's *A Book of Trout Flies,* truly a landmark book. Jennings enlisted the best aquatic entomologists of the era, illustrated the flies with exquisite watercolors, and utilized both his own patterns and other popular ones designed for eastern waters. The only problem was that the book was first published by Derrydale Press in a limited edition of 850 with hand-colored plates. It sold for $20, a nice chunk of change in 1935. Jennings enlisted some of the best fly fishers of the Catskill region to help him collect insects, including an innkeeper named Art Flick.

Flick's friend Ray Camp, who wrote the "Wood, Field & Stream" column for *The New York Times* in the 1930s, tried to convince him to write a book on fly hatches, but Flick wouldn't hear of it. I was lucky enough to spend an afternoon with Art Flick in the 1980s and he explained his reluctance: "For God's sake, I got one year of high school. How the hell am I ever going to write a book and do it justice?" Flick also felt an allegiance to Jennings and thought it would be plagiarism. But Camp didn't agree, as Flick remembered him saying:

> I'm talking about a book for fishermen. Jennings's book is for writers and people who appreciate artwork. I want you to do a book that a person could put in his pocket and take out on a stream and use, really use. Now can you picture them taking a $20 book down on the stream and comparing flies?

Flick dithered some more and kept coming up with excuses. Finally, Camp threatened to end their friendship if Flick didn't write the book. Flick agreed and the common man soon had a guide to trout-stream insects that was inexpensive and could be kept in a fishing jacket for reference.

Stripped Hackle Stem Bodies

You sometimes hear derisive comments about Catskill flies and their use of esoteric materials—like the Rhode Island Red stripped hackle quills used on the Red Quill or urine-burned belly hair from a vixen fox—as if they were some form of elitist fly tier snobbery. Nothing could be further from the truth. Flick was an innkeeper and hunter and trapper and lived in the country. He didn't have access to packaged fly materials or fancy dyes. Flick was using the best materials he could find in his limited rural environment. He was probably looking over a fox pelt from a local trapper when he noticed the fur on the underside of a female fox was the perfect pinkish tannish gray of the female *Ephemerella subvaria* mayfly. He wasn't trying to be cute, or to send tiers on campaigns scouring the countryside for material that is difficult to obtain.

In the same way, he noticed that when he stripped the quill from a local barnyard rooster it made the perfect imitation of a rusty mayfly body. He thought he was the first one to use stripped hackle quills for fly bodies, although recent evidence suggests that English tiers were using stripped hackle quills as early as the 1880s. But that particular color cannot be found on any other chicken feather, as the brown hackle capes we use today have either white- or black-edged stems and are nowhere near as deep in color. Other hackle stems can be dyed to a rusty red color, but if you can find someone who raises Rhode Island Red chickens—or find the rare one in a Catskill fly shop through an Internet search as I did recently—it's definitely worth the effort.

Hackle stems are not as popular for fly bodies as they should be. They are durable and lifelike. Very few materials give the same insect-like segmentation, and every tier has a pile of big feathers from the top of a hackle cape that are worthless for anything else. Flick used hackle stems not only for his Red Quill, but also for his two favorite dry flies, the Dun Variant and the Grey Fox Variant. Any color hackle stem can be used, and if you can't find the right color (you have to strip the stem first before you can see what color it will be when wound), hackle stems can be dyed using standard household clothing dyes.

Hackle stems should be soaked in water overnight at the very least, but I find a mixture of hair conditioner and water makes them less likely to split when wound. I usually just dump the entire contents of a hotel conditioner bottle (because my wife tells me not to use her "good stuff") into a large water glass. You could probably get away with less. I make bodies from a Rhode Island Red cape that is close to 50 years old and with this treatment even those old brittle feathers don't break when I wind them.

On the left is a Rhode Island Red hackle cape as seen from the back side. The presence of red web right down to the base of the stem indicates the quills will have a rusty red color when stripped and wound. In contrast, most brown necks today, as seen on the right, have white or black web at the base and the resulting stripped quills won't show the deep rusty color.

1 ■ Prepare a bunch of red quill hackle bodies the day before tying a Red Quill. Strip the fibers carefully from as much of the stem as you can, and soak them in a mixture of hair conditioner and water.

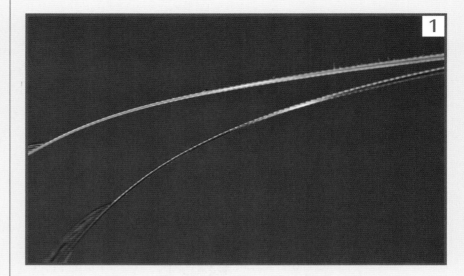

2 ■ Start your thread in the middle of the hook shank and wrap back smoothly with non-overlapping turns until the thread is hanging right above the point of the barb of the hook. Because this fly will have a hackle quill body, take more care to wrap a smooth base than you normally would. You can cover up an uneven underbody with fur or peacock herl, but quill bodies don't tolerate any inconsistencies underneath.

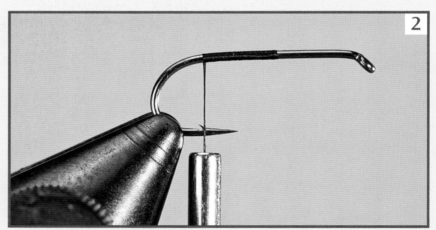

3 ■ Find a spade hackle at the side of a dark blue dun hackle cape with long, stiff, glossy barbs. Hold the tip of the feather with the thumb and forefinger of your left hand while bracing the bottom of the feather from behind with the pinkie of the same hand. This makes it easy to grab the tail fibers by pulling about 20 fibers perpendicular to the stem with the thumb and forefinger of your right hand. When the fibers are lined up, twitch them from the stem with a quick snap. Cut the very bottoms of the tail fibers off to even up the ends. This also makes the fibers lie straight when you tie them in.

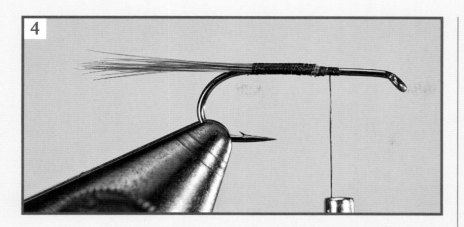

4 ◾ Measure the tail fibers so they are as long as the shank of the hook. Angle the butts slightly toward you and wrap over them to the middle of the shank, moving them in line with the shank as you tie them in. This helps the fibers lie straight on top of the hook. Trim any remaining tail fibers in the middle of the shank. You don't have to trim them at an angle because they are not bulky like hair tails.

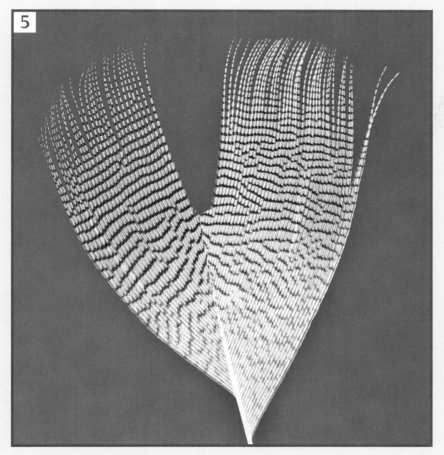

5 ◾ Wind the thread to just shy of the eye and then back to a point one-quarter of the way back from the eye. Select a large flank feather from a drake wood duck with symmetrical fibers on either side of the shank. (If you don't have any of these, you can use shorter or non-symmetrical feathers, but you will have to prepare two bunches and then combine them to get enough for a wing.) Strip all of the down and any shorter fibers from both sides of the feather. Snip the center stem out of the feather about halfway down from the tips with the point of your scissors and save this for nymph legs.

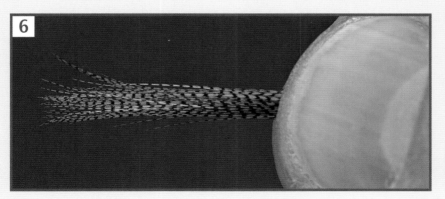

6 ◾ Without removing the fibers from the stem, manipulate them so the tips are even, and then cut the fibers from the stem. Keep them pinched between your fingers slightly so they stay aligned. Don't even think of trying to stack wood duck wing fibers in a stacker—they're too fine and it won't work—so pay careful attention to their alignment before you cut them from the stem.

7 ■ Measure the wing against the shank—it should be the length of the hook shank from the tie-in point to the tips of the fibers. Tie in the wing with about four tight turns of thread—wood duck does not need much to secure it and you want to avoid bulk around the wings.

8 ■ Trim the butts of the fibers at a taper that ends where the tail fibers were cut off. This gives you a smooth base for the hackle quill body.

9 ■ Raise the wings straight up and secure them in the upright position with about six tight turns of thread right up against the front of the wing.

10 ▪ Separate the wing into two equal bunches with a dubbing needle.

11 ▪ Make a figure-eight wrap through the wings by winding between the wings on top from front to back while holding onto the near wing, under the hook shank, and then between the wings from back to front while holding onto the far wing. It should take only a single figure-eight wrap to divide them, which also eliminates bulk. I have seen some tiers "post" their wood duck wings by wrapping a couple of turns around their bases. However, Catskill tiers like Flick did not post their wings, I think for good reason, because it makes the fine wood duck fibers too condensed and thin, which keeps their fine speckling from showing through the entire upper part of the hackle. If any fibers are truly out of line, trim them carefully at the base of the wing.

12 ▪ Take the thread back a few turns behind the wing. Tie in a well-soaked Rhode Island Red hackle stem by the tip. Wind back to the tail, keeping the stem on top of the hook shank so you don't get any off-center lumps when you wind it back forward. Bring the thread back to a point just behind the wings.

13 ■ Wind the hackle stem forward with turns that touch the preceding one closely enough that the tying thread does not show through, but not close enough that they overlap. When you get about one turn from the end, carefully pinch the stem close to the hook to flatten it, which helps you tie it in without bulk. Secure the hackle stem with about four tight turns of thread and snip it as close to the hook shank as possible. Bind under any part of the stem that sticks up, as anything that sticks up will prevent you from winding your hackles smoothly and evenly. Leave the thread hanging right up against the last turn of quill.

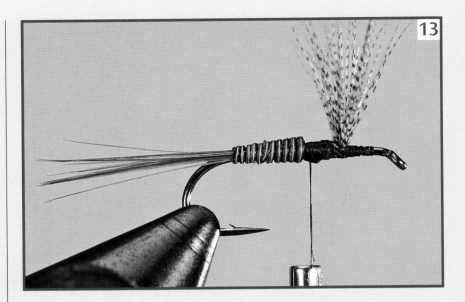

14 ■ Select two long, densely fibered dark dun neck hackles with fibers that are between one-and-a-half and two times the hook gape. Strip the stems where the webby fibers at the base are found. A little web in the center of a dry-fly hackle is OK, but make sure anything you leave is no more than 10 percent web. Place the hackles so their concave sides face each other.

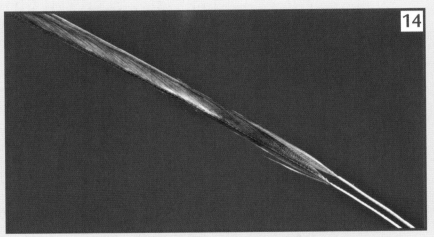

15 ■ Tie in the hackle stems flat on top of the hook shank, placing the butt ends between the wings. Wind forward, leaving a smooth base for the hackle. When the thread gets to the wing, jump in front of the wings and bind down a short section of the hackle butts in front of the wing as well. This gives you a smoother base for winding hackle and helps secure them better. Trim the hackle stems a few turns of thread short of the eye.

16 ▪ Grab the hackles with your fingers and begin winding forward. Try to hold them close to their bases so the hackle stems stay close together. You will probably get two turns of hackle behind the wings; then, pull the wings out of the way and bring the hackles tight to the front of the wings, with their fibers staying as perpendicular to the hook shank as possible. You will probably get two more turns in front of the wing.

17 ▪ Tie off the hackles by holding them almost straight up and just angled far enough forward to catch their bases with the thread. Tie them off with about four tight turns of thread. Trim the hackles very close to the hook shank and wrap a few more tight turns over them and forward to just behind the eye to get a neat head. Whip finish.

18 ▪ With a fine-pointed dubbing needle, coat the quill body carefully with deep-penetrating head cement, letting just a tiny bit of head cement seep into the back of the hackle winds. Add a single drop of head cement to the bare thread winds at the head. After the body dries, you may wish to add a second coat of head cement for extra durability.

The Royal Wulff, known by most as a prototypical western dry fly, actually evolved gradually in the New York City area and can trace its lineage back to the 19th century. And although it carries the name of one of the most iconic fly-fishing innovators of all time, Lee Wulff, the original hair-winged Royal Coachman was developed under the direction of a man with a much less romantic name. And Wulff himself was not the actual inventor of the pattern.

The original Coachman fly was an English wet fly tied with duck quill wings, brown hackle, and a peacock herl body. The way the Royal variation came about was first documented by Mary Orvis Marbury in her landmark 1892 book, *Favorite Flies and Their Histories*, the first catalog of American fly patterns. In the section on the Royal Coachman, Marbury describes how John Haily, a New York City fly dresser, first tied the fly for a man who wanted some Coachman patterns for north woods fishing, but he asked for a more durable solution to the fragile peacock herl. Haily added a red silk band in the middle of the fly, and further completed the transformation with strongly barred wood duck flank feather fibers (not the golden pheasant tippets commonly used on the "traditional" Royal Coachman used in the

■ Lee Wulff

Hook
Standard dry fly, sizes 8–18

Thread
Black 8/0

Tail
Brown bucktail

Body
Peacock herl with red floss band
in the middle

Wing
White bucktail, calf tail, or
calf body hair

Hackle
Brown

the founder of The Orvis Company, said, "Oh, it is easy enough. Call it the Royal Coachman, it is so finely dressed."

When the dry-fly craze overtook American fly fishers in the early 20th century, it was natural that this popular wet fly was modified as a dry fly. It was tied with slips of white duck quill, but over time some tiers substituted wide white breast feathers from a wood duck, and that fly was christened the Fanwing Royal Coachman. Although the fanwing was a deadly pattern and highly visible in fast water, the delicate white feather wings were fragile and lost their shape once the fly was drowned by a fish. Leonard Quackenbush, a member of the Beaverkill Trout Club in the Catskills, asked legendary Catskill fly tier Reuben Cross to develop a more durable pattern and Cross substituted wings of white impala hair and tails of brown hackle fibers. Cross named his new fly the Quack.

At about the same time, a couple of fishing buddies named Dan Bailey and Lee Wulff were tying flies for their favorite rivers in the Adiron-

20th century). A few evenings after he first tied the new fly, some tiers were discussing a name for it, and L.C. Orvis, brother of Charles F. Orvis,

The tumbling West Branch of the Ausable River in the Adirondacks was the birthplace of the Wulff dry flies.

dacks, Catskills, and Vermont. Wulff was already famous for his bulky hair wing flies: the Gray Wulff was tied to imitate various dark mayflies that hatched on the foaming waters of the Ausable River in the Adirondacks, while the White Wulff was tied to mimic the spinner of the green drake mayfly in fast water. Wulff used hair for both wings and tails, and Bailey suggested that he also tie a variation of the Quack Coachman, so Wulff tied some of the flies with brown bucktail tails instead of the brown hackle fibers used on the Quack. Later, Bailey, who began his career as a physicist, moved to Montana and started the eponymous fly shop in Livingston and began marketing the fly as the Royal Wulff.

Wulff later put his career as an artist on hold and became synonymous with wilderness fishing for brook trout and Atlantic salmon, based on publicity arrangements with Newfoundland and Labrador in Canada. He invented the fishing vest as we know it today. He conceived of the idea of a fly reel that could be palmed to increase drag without the need to adjust a screw or lever. He codified our concept of catch-and-release fishing with his statement in 1938:

> There is a growing tendency among anglers to release their fish, returning them to the water in order that they may furnish sport again for a brother angler. Game fish are too valuable to be caught only once.

He caught marlin with a fly rod and single-action freshwater reel from a small boat. He became the hero of every American boy who stayed glued to the television each weekend to catch the next episode of *The American Sportsman*. But the way he is most remembered in the 21st century is the concatenation of his name to a fly he did not develop. Nevertheless, it's a fitting tribute to the man to whom today's fly fishers owe so much.

Pattern Variations

ROYAL TRUDE

Hook: Standard dry fly, sizes 8–18
Thread: Black 8/0
Tail: Golden pheasant tippet
Body: Peacock herl with red floss band in the middle
Wing: White calf tail, tied down flat over body and not divided
Hackle: Brown

ROYAL HUMPY

Hook: Standard dry fly or Bigeye hook in smaller sizes
Thread: Red 6/0
Tail: Moose body hair
Wing and Body Overlay: Large bunch of long, coarse, hollow elk hair from a calf or bull elk
Hackle: Brown
  ■ Long, narrow, domestic saddles are best, but long neck hackles can also be used.

Choosing Wings for Visible Flies

ee Wulff preferred bucktail for the wings on his Wulff dry flies, but admitted they did not look as good as other hairs. It's worth noting that Wulff used his hair wing dry flies for Atlantic salmon as much as trout, and for the bigger Atlantic salmon dries, bucktail is perfect for making a substantial wing. For the smaller trout flies used today, bucktail is too coarse and does not make the neat wing acceptable to modern tiers.

There is a natural tendency to use fine white synthetic nylon fibers for hair wing flies. They are durable, easy to find, and easy to use. However, synthetics make horrible wings when compared to hair. They mat too easily when wet, are too soft, and don't retain their shape after numerous false casts. Natural hairs give us the right amount of stiffness and water repellency, plus the finely tapered tips that, although not necessary for an effective fly, look better in our view of how a dry fly should appear in the vise or in the bins of a fly shop.

The original hair for the Quack Coachman was white impala hair, probably widely available in the early 20th century when big-game hunters were imitating Theodore Roosevelt's African hunting expeditions. However, white calf tail hair became the accepted hair for dry-fly wings, to the point where it is often called "impala" by fly-tying suppliers. Calf tail is durable, has a nice glossy sheen, and has a slight crimp that enables the wing to hold more air bubbles when drowned, thus giving a dry fly better floating qualities. When choosing calf tail for tying dry flies, pick a tail without a strong curl in the fibers, as some tails are so kinky that it is difficult to find hair straight enough to make wings. The coarser hair near the base of the tail is also straighter and more substantial than the finer hair at the tip.

White calf body hair is also used for wings on dry flies, and it looks better on a finished fly, especially on hooks smaller than size 12. Calf body stacks neatly and is finer than calf tail so it offers less bulk at the base of the wings. However, because calf body is finer and straighter than calf tail, it has a tendency to mat when wet and as a result the finished wing should be tied bulkier to get the same wide profile for visibility.

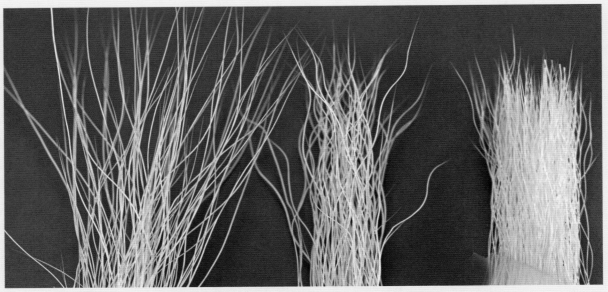

Three types of hair that can be used for white wings on dry flies. Bucktail, on the left, is not used often because it is difficult to even the ends in a stacker and it's very stiff. Calf tail, in the middle, resists water because of its slight curl and is the most popular material used today. Calf body, on the right, is easy to stack and makes very neat wings, especially on smaller flies.

1 ■ Cut a fairly large bunch of brown bucktail from the back side of a natural tail. First, remove shorter fibers from the bucktail by holding the tips tightly and pulling on the bottom of the hair bunch. Even it in a stacker. It helps to cut the bucktail shorter than the stacker height before stacking, and you might even want to stack one bunch, put it aside, stack a second bunch, combine the two bunches, and stack a third and final time.

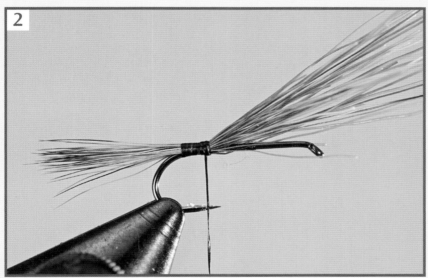

2 ■ Tie the bucktail in by holding it at a slight angle to the shank, with the butt ends angled slightly toward the near side of the hook shank and the tail ends pointing slightly away from you. When you begin winding thread over them, the tails should align neatly on top of the hook shank. Wind forward about one-third of the way to the eye of the hook.

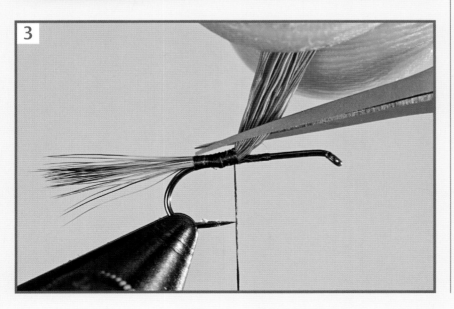

3 ■ Lift the butt ends of the tails off the hook and trim them on a slight bias. The angle of the bias will meet an opposite angle on the wing butts and you will get a relatively smooth underbody, which can be further smoothed out with thread.

4 ■ Advance the thread to just shy of the eye of the hook and then return the thread to a distance about one-quarter of the way back from the eye.

5 ■ Cut a bunch of calf tail or body hair that is about 75 percent more than you think you need. You will lose a lot of it when cleaning the shorter hairs and fuzz from the base, and Wulff wings should be relatively bulky anyway. (Wings that are too wimpy will mat and you won't be able to see them on the water.) Hold the hairs one-quarter of the way down from their tips, pinch this spot with your thumb and forefinger, and pull firmly with your other fingers to remove all short hairs and fuzz from the base of the hair. Place the hair in a large-diameter stacker. Stack the hair by rapping it with a firm staccato motion. Too hard of a stacking motion makes the hair jump up and move out of alignment, but if you don't use enough force the hair won't fall to the bottom. Open the stacker and check the hairs. If they aren't perfectly even, shove them gently back inside, twirl the sides of the stacker a bit to jostle them, and rap them again until they are very even when you open the stacker.

6 ■ Measure the wing against the shank of the hook. It should be as long as the entire shank before the bend. Tie in the hair with five to six very firm winds, using only upward and downward pressure to keep the hair from rolling over the side of the hook. It also helps to pinch the sides of the hook when you tighten. If the hair bunch rolls to the far side, back up a couple of turns, roll the hair back on top of the hook, and wrap again.

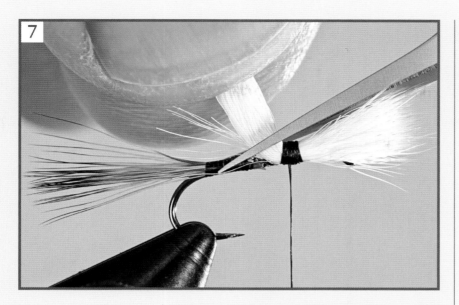

7 ■ Lift the hair at a 45-degree angle above the horizontal and trim the hair on a bias so it roughly matches the tail cut in a mirror image. As long as it's close, you'll be fine.

8 ■ Wrap back over the cut ends of the hair to firmly secure it. Bring the thread back in front of the wing. The rear two-thirds of the body should be flat with no taper; there will be a slight buildup behind the wing because it's bulkier than the tail, but you'll cover that with the front herl section and the hackle winds.

9 ■ Hold the wing straight up and wrap a dam of thread right up against it. Use firm thread tension and stop when the wing stands up on its own.

10 ■ Separate the wing into two equal bunches with a dubbing needle. Make two figure-eight wraps by winding between the wings on top from front to back while holding onto the near wing, under the hook shank, and then between the wings from back to front while holding onto the far wing. If any hairs stick way out of place at this point (it's especially common on the far side of the wing), trim them carefully right at the base. Any wild hairs are not going to get more manageable, especially when you're winding hackle, so it's a good idea to get rid of them right now.

11 ■ Take two turns of thread around the base of the far wing. Wind one turn around the shank and then take two turns of thread around the base of the near wing. In this case, use light thread tension, just enough to bring all the wing fibers together at the base. If you put too much tension on these wraps, the thread will creep up the wings and those black winds over white wings will show up in the finished fly. And no brown trout more than six inches long will ever take your fly when it sees how sloppy it is. (If you want to get really fancy, you can tie the fly with white thread up to this point, then whip finish and switch to black thread.) Trim any stray wing fibers again. It's not a bad idea to place a tiny drop of head cement at the base of each wing.

12 ■ Take the thread back to the base of the tail. Tie in two narrow herls from the base of a small peacock eye, or four fibers from the top of the feather (right above the iridescent eye). Tie the peacock herl in by their tips with two tight turns of thread. Trim them as close to the shank as possible and advance the thread toward the eye just two turns. Take two turns with the peacock herl and tie off with another two tight turns of thread. Trim the peacock as close to the hook shank as you can. Peacock does not take many turns of thread to secure, thus you can avoid bulk in the body easily.

13 ■ Bring the thread forward to the halfway point on the hook shank. Take a single strand of red floss and tie it in on top of the hook with just two turns of thread, but don't trim the end. Wind the floss smoothly back to meet the herl and then wind back to the starting point. If the body does not look smooth back up and start again, and be very careful of the hook point—it can easily fray the floss. Tie off the floss with two turns of thread and now trim both ends.

14 ■ Advance the thread forward two turns. Tie in the same number of herls you used for the rear portion with two turns toward the rear and then bring the thread forward two turns. Take two turns with the peacock herl and tie it off with two turns. It should just slightly cover the front portion of the red floss so no black thread shows through. Wind a few turns of thread in back of the wing to form a smooth, even base for the hackle.

15 ■ Select two brown saddle or neck hackles with dense, even fibers and thin stems. The fibers of the hackles should be between one-and-a-half and twice the length of the hook gape. Trim the fibers at the base very close to the stems. Place the two feathers together so that the concave sides are facing each other.

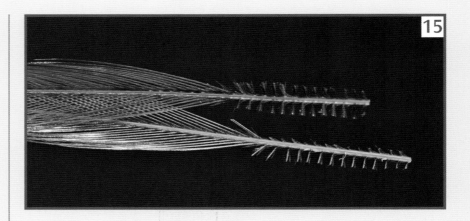

16 ■ Tie in the two feathers together behind the wing, with the stems laid between the wings. Leave a small bit of stripped stem beyond the thread so your first turn of hackle won't angle it back over the body. Advance the thread forward to the base of the wing. Trim the part of the stems that extend beyond the front of the wing. Bring the thread in front of the wing and wind back and forth a few times in front of the wing to even up the base for the hackle. Because the base behind the wing is bulkier than that in front, the hackle likes to jump out of place as you wind it forward. You shouldn't try to get as much bulk in front of the wings as behind, but evening the jump a bit helps.

17 ■ Grab both hackles together and make one wind tight up against the peacock herl. Make one or two more turns behind the wing, working slightly forward as you do. The hackle should look dense, but it shouldn't be packed in so tightly that it begins to flare in all directions.

18 ■ Use your fingers to pull the wing back out of the way and make a single turn of hackle right up against the base of the wing. Be careful to keep the hackle perpendicular to the hook shank when you do this; otherwise, the hackle will stick out over the eye, making it tough to make the next turn of hackle without binding some fibers under and making it tough to finish off the head without tying in the fibers that stick out over the eye. Take one or two more turns of hackle, working slightly forward with each turn as you did behind the wing.

19 ■ Don't wind all the way to the eye. Stop just short of it. Hold the hackles at 45-degree angles above the hook shank, pointing slightly away from you, and tie in the ends of the hackle with four or five very tight turns of thread. If you hold the hackle at just the right angle, all the fibers will line up against the preceding turns and your finished fly will look clean and neat

20 ■ Trim the hackles close to the shank. Wind a neat head until all the ends of the hackles are bound under. Apply a drop or two of deep-penetrating head cement, allowing it to seep back slightly onto the bases of the closest hackle winds for added security. The Royal Wulff is one tough pattern to create and you don't want yours to fall apart after only a couple of fish!

7 Sparkle Dun

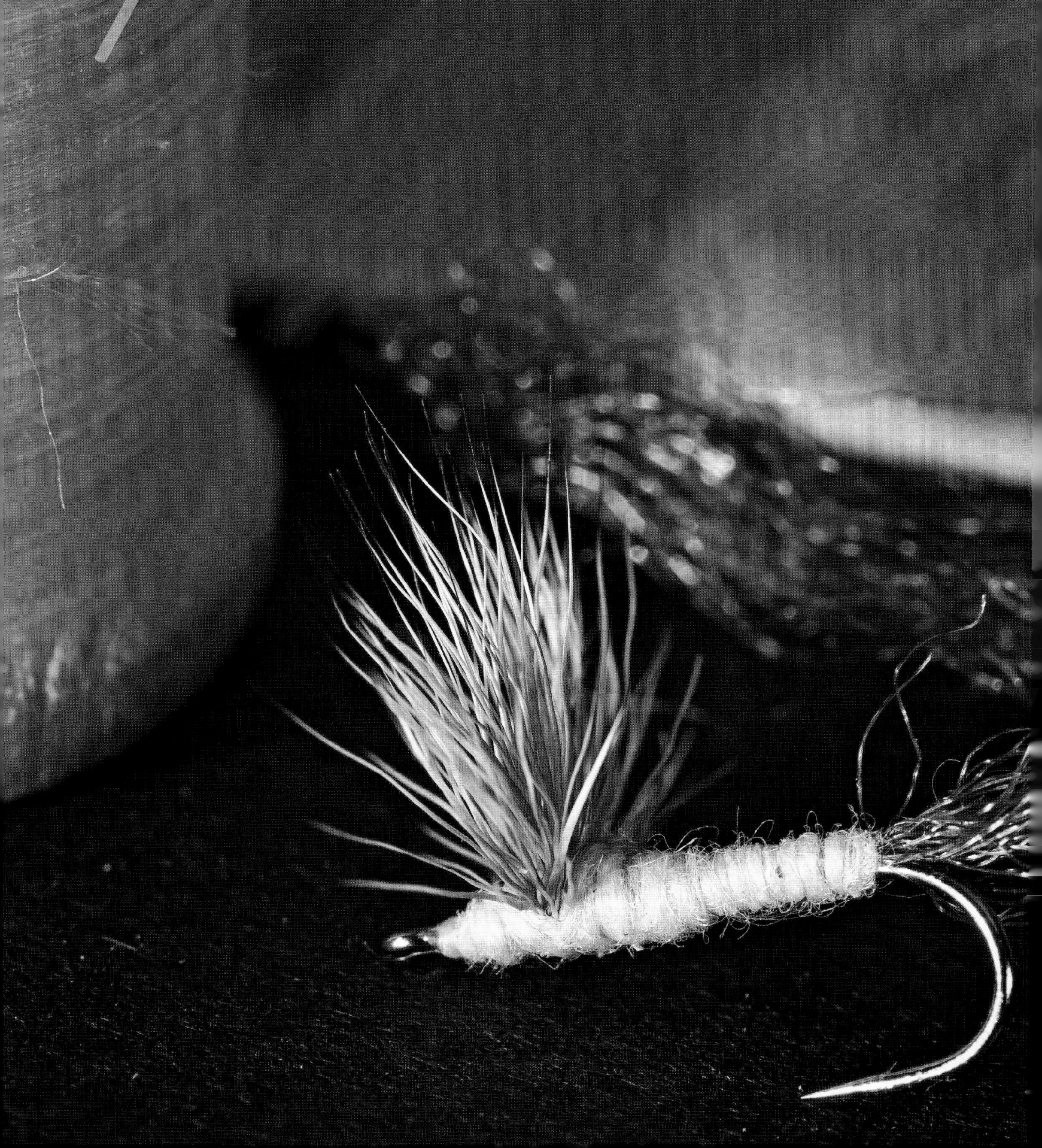

The PMD, or Pale Morning Dun, is an angler's popular term for a group of mayflies that hatches in trout waters west of the Mississippi River from late spring through late summer. The scientific names of these mayflies are *Ephemerella inermis* and *Ephemerella infrequens*, at least those identified by anglers, but there may be other species that fit the same behavior and general appearance that have not been identified yet. They can be annoying little bugs. Although these small, size 16 through 22 mayflies bring trout to the surface in great numbers, they also make trout that are normally just casually selective into gourmands that seem to take issue with every bite. No one knows why, but it is probably because PMD hatches can last for weeks and even months on any given water, and when trout eat the same insect every day, they get pretty certain about their next mouthful. Anything that doesn't match their search image perfectly gets ignored.

PMDs show a very subtle coloration, and the adults have wings that are not quite cream and not quite gray, with yellowish bodies tinged with orange or olive. Water chemistry probably influences the exact coloration; the PMDs on the Madison River in Montana have an olive cast, but if your PMD imitations on the South Fork of the Snake in Idaho don't have a tinge of orange, the big fussy cutthroats that poke their noses

Craig Matthews

into shallow riffles to feed on these mayflies may ignore your best presentation.

It was this little mayfly that drove Yellowstone anglers Craig Matthews and John Juracek to develop their Sparkle Dun pattern, which is perhaps the most popular and effective imitation of an emerging mayfly ever developed. In 1983, during the heyday of the large surface-feeding rainbow trout of the Henry's Fork of the Snake in Idaho, Matthews and Juracek were frustrated by rainbows eating PMD mayflies. The fish seemed to be selecting mayflies that still had the nymph shuck attached to the backs of their abdomens and ignoring the fully emerged, fluttering duns—which makes sense because a mayfly struggling to shimmy out of its former home won't take off and fly away anytime soon. The emerging flies were easy prey.

For the chassis of the fly, both Matthews and Juracek liked an upright wing made out of deer hair, without hackle, and with a dubbed body.

Pattern Description

Hook
Standard dry fly, sizes 16–20

Thread
Yellow 6/0

Tail (Shuck)
Brown Z-Lon, full strand on size 16, partial strand on smaller sizes

Body
Pale yellow superfine synthetic dubbing (original pattern used rabbit fur, which is also excellent)
Add a touch of orange or olive dubbing to match local color variations of the PMD.

Wing
Fine, even hair from a whitetail deer

Pattern Variations

HAYSTACK
Hook: Standard dry fly, sizes 8–12
Thread: Fluorescent orange 3/0
Tail: Thick bunch of deer hair
Body: Tan Australian opossum fur
Wing: Thick bunch of deer hair, not stacked, and tied in so that it stands upright and flares 180 degrees over the hook

PMD COMPARADUN
Hook: Standard dry fly, sizes 16–20
Thread: Yellow 6/0
Tail: Light blue dun hackle fibers, split around a small ball of dubbing so they splay 90 degrees
Body: Pale yellow rabbit fur dubbing
  ▪ Add a touch of orange or olive dubbing to match local color variations of the PMD.
Wing: Fine, even hair of a pale shade from the face of a whitetail deer

This part of the fly design was not new. In 1949, Francis Betters, the most famous Adirondack fly tier of the 20th century, developed a pattern called the Haystack while still in high school. It was not a pretty imitation of any specific mayfly; in fact, it was designed to imitate the profile of lots of different aquatic insects on the tumbling, foamy waters of the West Branch of the Ausable River in Wilmington, New York. Betters tied it with a large hunk of deer hair for the tail, a body dubbed from muskrat or possum fur, and a large, scraggly wing of coarse deer belly hair that was so massive it spilled over the sides of the fly and

helped stabilize it in the water. Betters used it as large as a size 6.

During the hatch-matching renaissance of the 1970s, other fly tiers took notice of the hair-winged dry fly without hackle. Doug Swisher and Carl Richards, in their innovative 1971 book *Selective Trout*—which introduced the concept of a fly with no hackle to a broad audience—showed a drawing of a prototypical hair-winged no-hackle fly, but it didn't seem to catch on. It wasn't until the publication of *Hatches* by Al Caucci and Bob Nastasi in 1975 that the concept of a mayfly imitation with hair wings and no hackle caught

Selecting Hair for Sparkle Duns

The most important part of tying the Sparkle Dun comes well before thread is ever applied to the hook. Without the proper hair, the Sparkle Dun is difficult to tie, doesn't look right, and won't catch as many fish. To tie it properly, a fly tier must obtain fine, even hair and the black tips on the hair must be short in relation to the rest of the hair. Otherwise, the hair will not flare properly. Al Caucci and Bob Nastasi recommended hair from the face of a whitetail deer, but Craig Matthews felt hair from the face was poor compared to fine hair from the flanks, neck, and upper leg. Belly or back hair from a whitetail flares too much and the fibers are too coarse to give a good wing profile. Hair from mule deer (or its subspecies, the coastal blacktail deer) does not flare properly and the black tips are too long. Elk is too coarse and also does not flare well. Caribou flares too much, doesn't line up neatly in a finished fly, and is so brittle that it breaks after a few fish.

If you buy hair through the mail, ask for Sparkle Dun hair or Comparadun hair. If you pick out the hair yourself in a fly shop, which is always better, look for hair that is fine but still hollow so that it flares (some deer hair is so fine that is almost looks like fur and does not flare at all); tips

that are short and barely have any black in them; and fibers that line up neatly on the hide. If you are a deer hunter or know someone who is, you should know that Craig Matthews prefers hair from a deer killed in October from a cold climate. Avoid hair that is too coarse, has long, stringy black tips, or ends that don't look even. Hair used for tying bass flies and Muddler Minnows just won't cut it. I have special bags of this hair that I treasure more than my finest hackle. When you see a good piece of Sparkle Dun hair, buy it.

■ Only the deer hair on the left will make a good Sparkle Dun. The hair in the middle and on the right has long, black tips and is too coarse for a Sparkle Dun. Save these for Muddler heads and bass bugs.

on with a broad group of anglers and fly tiers. Caucci and Nastasi, describing the genesis of their Comparadun flies, gave credit to Betters for the concept, but they neatened up the fly considerably, making the body and wing outline cleaner and replacing the bulky hair tails with delicate split tails of hackle fibers, more in line with the precise imitation philosophy of the day. Very important to the construction of their Comparadun was the use of fine hair from the face of a white-tail deer, which allowed the creation of smaller flies without bulk, gave the fly a great outline, and aided flotation.

Matthews and Juracek felt that the flimsy tails used in the Comparadun weren't substantial enough for the tumbling waters of most Rocky Mountain streams, and they still wanted to imitate that trailing shuck. They tried various options for the shuck, including sections of feathers and marabou, but noticed these opaque materials didn't imitate the shimmering, sparkling shuck well enough. They remembered that Gary LaFontaine, in his monumental book *Caddisflies*, used Antron yarn for his Sparkle Pupa to imitate the shuck around a natural caddis pupa. But they weren't happy with Antron for a shuck; although they liked its sparkle, the fibers tended to mat together when wet and trapped the algae so common on the surface of the Henry's Fork.

They had recently obtained some samples of a material called Z-Lon from innovative Denver fly tier John Betts, who had initially found it on the inside of boot laces. Like Antron, Z-Lon is a trilobal nylon fiber, which gives it sparkle, but it has more of a kink in it, which is better to trap air bubbles and prevent matting. Matthews and Juracek found in Z-Lon the perfect material to complete the effect they wanted in their Sparkle Dun.

The Sparkle Dun became an overwhelming success in the summer of 1983, and is still, a decade into the 21st century, the most popular imitation of the PMD mayfly, as well as many others. During one of the fly's early years, Matthews and Juracek were fishing at the upper fence line on the Railroad Ranch section of the Henry's Fork and were just pounding the fish on Sparkle Duns. Standing on the bank was the legendary Ernest Schwiebert, at the time perhaps the most famous trout angler in the world and a man not known to ask *anyone* what fly they were using, but finally he blurted out, "What the hell kind of fly are you guys using?" The fate of the Sparkle Dun was sealed.

■ The rich, flat water of the Henry's Fork and its fussy trout led to the development of the Sparkle Dun.

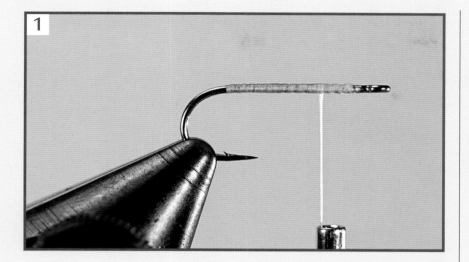

1 ■ Cover the hook shank from just behind the eye to the bend with tying thread. After covering the hook shank, bring the thread to a point that is one-third of the way back from the eye.

2 ■ Cut a section of deer hair from the hide that is about the same diameter as the hook gape (the vertical distance between the point of the hook and the shank). Hold the hair by the tips and pull any short hairs or soft underfur from the bunch. Place the hair in a stacker and rap sharply four to six times to even the ends of the hair. Lay the hair over the top of the hook and reposition the hair in your fingers until your thumb and forefinger just begin to cover the hair at a distance of one hook-shank length from the tips. Place this point over the thread position and take one loose turn over the hair. Pinch tightly against the sides of the hook so that the hair does not roll off and take a second tight turn of thread in the same spot. Take about four more tight turns over the hair, working just slightly back away from the eye with each subsequent turn.

3 ■ Lift the butt ends of the hair up slightly and trim them at an angle. Wind thread tightly over the butt ends of the hair. These turns must be tight to secure the hair and to avoid making a large lump behind the wing, but the wing also tends to roll over on the near side when you do this. Try to make these turns with upward and downward pressure rather than rolling the thread around the butt ends of the hair. Trim any hairs that are out of place and fuss with the clump of hair until it is distributed around the top 180 degrees of the hook shank, not below it.

4 ■ Grab one-half or one-third of the wing clump with your thumb and forefinger and raise it upright. Make about six tight turns immediately in front of this clump. Repeat the process once or twice until all the hair has been raised upright.

5 ■ Make some extra turns in front of the wing to ensure that it stays up. (Originally, on the Comparaduns and the original Sparkle Duns, the wing clump was raised upright in a single unit and a large bump of thread was built up in front of the wing. One day about 10 years ago, Matthews and Juracek were messing around in their fly shop, Blue Ribbon Flies, and they played with the idea of raising the clump in several stages. Not only is this method more durable and less bulky, but the wing is also less likely to slant forward a few days after the fly is tied, and the finished wing has more of a three-dimensional shape.)

6 ■ Bring the thread back behind the wing and catch the piece of Z-Lon under the thread at the point where the wing butts end. This will ensure a smooth body that imitates the shape of the natural mayfly.

7 ■ Wind the thread back over the Z-Lon to the bend of the hook. Cut the tail or shuck so that it is slightly shorter than the hook shank; if left longer, it tends to catch around the hook bend when cast. Trim the trailing end of the shuck so that it is tapered by taking small, short cuts along the side to imitate the tapered shape of the natural nymph shuck.

8 ■ Dub a thin amount of dubbing to the tying thread, in a short taper that is thin closest to the hook shank and just slightly thicker as it gets closer to the bobbin. None of the dubbing should be applied thickly, as the thorax already has more bulk and you will take several turns of dubbing around it to build it up a bit more.

9 ■ Before winding the body all the way forward, inspect your wing from the front to make sure that it is fully upright and that it splays 180 degrees across the upper part of the fly. This will help balance the fly on the water and will imitate both the legs and the wings of the fly. Wind the dubbing in tight turns from the base of the shuck toward the wing. If the body develops gaps, angle the dubbing back a bit toward the bend. If the body develops lumps, apply more pressure to the thread.

10 ■ When you reach the wing, leave a slight gap of dubbing behind it and pull the wing upright and back slightly while winding the dubbing tight up against the wing. Make another wind of dubbing behind the wing, then wind forward to just behind the eye. Try to get a nice taper in front of the wing, either by winding tighter as you get closer to the eye, or by backing up, removing a bit of dubbing, spinning what is left back onto the thread, and then winding forward. With a very sparse amount of dubbing, you can wind back and forth several times until you can finish with that final wind just behind the eye.

11 ■ Whip finish and apply a drop of head cement to the bare thread left by the whip finish.

8 Stimulator

You can tell a fly has reached the zenith of popularity when guides give it a nickname. "You try a Stimmy yet?" is the call often made from one drift boat to another when the fish turn off their feeding for reasons beyond our comprehension. I was a latecomer to the magic of the Stimulator, and avoided it for years because I had not intercepted many large stone fly hatches. I guess it struck me one day on Colorado's South Platte River, where the typical day involves hanging size 22 or 24 midge nymphs off a strike indicator, and if you're lucky, a size 20 olive mayfly might make an appearance. I was fishing with Monroe Coleman, a veteran guide and dry-fly maniac. "Dry or die" is usually the slogan we yell from one side of the river to another. It was a painfully bright day and the fish were snotty.

"Think I should try 8X?" I asked.

"Why don't you just dump your whole fly box in the river and save yourself the trouble?" Coleman replied. "I'm going to cut back my tippet to 4X and try a Stimmy."

I won't lie and tell you we caught a pile of fish that day, but just seeing those sophisticated South Platte rainbows and browns turn away from gobbling diminutive subsurface bugs and rise to the top for a fly that I had previously associated with big rocky freestone rivers and giant stone fly hatches was a revelation. Since my epiphany,

■ Randall Kaufmann

I've never gone anywhere without a Stimulator. I fish it in brawling Rocky Mountain rivers. I fish it in tiny brook-trout streams from North Carolina to Pennsylvania. I fish it for the educated brown trout on the Delaware River. Sometimes I think eastern trout anglers get too hung up on imitating what is on the water and forget that trout are opportunists, and as long as a big fly looks like something they've eaten over the past month, there is a chance a trout will rise to a big juicy imitation.

The Stimulator is the brainchild of Randall Kaufmann, originally from Oregon and now happily residing in Jackson Hole, Wyoming. Like many of the wildly popular fly patterns we use today, the Stimulator was an evolutionary fly. Kaufmann learned to fish in California, Oregon, Washington, Idaho, Wyoming, and Montana in the 1960s and '70s. There, big stone flies hatch all spring, followed by an abundance of large terrestrial insects, finishing the season with the large orange October Caddis. There were always big insects to imitate. As Kaufmann modestly told me:

> The Stimulator as a style of fly was not a new, nor unique design, but like most "new" flies it was built upon old ideas. There were several popular downwing patterns with similar "parts," including the Improved Sofa Pillow and the Royal Trude, both favorite flies of the day. I mixed the tying styles and replaced the "parts" with some of my favorite materials and colors to better represent the hatches that I fished.

But there is a difference between a novice fly tier changing a couple of materials on a fly pattern and adding his name to it and a veteran fly tier and highly perceptive and experienced angler like Randall Kaufmann. His tinkering is the process of careful experimentation and knowledge of exactly what a material substitution will do for a fly, in terms of its effectiveness, floating qualities, and durability. The Stimulator didn't arise fully formed

Pattern Description

Hook
Curved nymph hook, sizes 6–16

Thread
Fluorescent fire orange 6/0

Tail
Short, flared bunch of cow elk hair

Abdomen
Orange sparkle dubbing

Abdomen Hackle
Brown, short

Abdomen Rib
Fine gold wire

Wing
Cow elk hair, flared wide and tall

Thorax
Reddish orange sparkle dubbing

Thorax Hackle
Grizzly, slightly longer than abdomen hackle

An original Stimulator tied by Randall Kaufmann. Note how wide and tall his wing is, and how the tails have been spread. Most tiers (like me) make their Stimulators with more material so they look nicer, but Kaufmann feels they fish better when tied like this.

Pattern Variations

Note: Besides these variations in tying materials and profile, Stimulators are often tied in different colors as well. The more popular ones are green, tan, golden, black, and Royal (with a body like a Royal Wulff).

RUBBER-LEG CRYSTAL STIMULATOR, FLUORESCENT GREEN
(Sample tied by Randall Kaufmann)

Hook: Curved nymph hook, sizes 6–16

Thread: Fluorescent fire orange 6/0

Tail: Short, flared bunch of fluorescent green bull elk hair

Abdomen: Fluorescent green dubbing

Abdomen Hackle: Grizzly dyed pale olive

Abdomen Rib: Fine gold wire

Wing: Fluorescent green-dyed elk hair, topped with a small bunch of white calf tail for added visibility
  - Strands of multiple colors of Krystal Flash and Mirror Flash are tied in at each side of the wing.

Legs: Fluorescent green speckled rubber legs

Thorax: Pearlescent sparkle dubbing

Thorax Hackle: Grizzly, slightly longer than abdomen hackle

FOAMULATOR, BLACK
(Sample tied by Randall Kaufmann)

Hook: Curved nymph hook, sizes 6–16

Thread: Fluorescent fire orange 6/0

Tail: Trimmed piece of black foam overlay with iridescent top
  - Kaufmann prefers Northern Lights Loco Foam.

Overlay (Entire Fly): Black foam overlay with iridescent top
  - Kaufmann prefers Northern Lights Loco Foam.

Abdomen: Black dubbing
  - Kaufmann prefers Black Stimulator SLF.

Abdomen Hackle: Dark grizzly

Abdomen Rib: Fine gold wire

Wing: Black Web Wig under dyed chocolate brown elk and fluorescent hot pink yarn
  - A few strands of Krystal and Mirror Flash (multiple colors) are tied under the wing.

Legs: Black and white speckled rubber legs

Thorax: Pale pink sparkle dubbing
  - Kaufmann prefers Flame Stimulator SLF.

Thorax Hackle: Grizzly, slightly longer than abdomen hackle

ROYAL STIMULATOR
(Sample tied by Randall Kaufmann)

Hook: Curved nymph hook, sizes 6–16

Thread: Fluorescent fire orange 6/0

Tail: Short, flared bunch of cow elk hair

Abdomen: Pink sparkle dubbing with a band of peacock herl at each end
  - Kaufmann prefers Flame Stimulator SLF.

Abdomen Hackle: Brown, short

Abdomen Rib: Fine gold wire

Wing: Cow elk hair, flared wide and tall, over a few strands of Krystal and Mirror Flash (multiple colors)
  - A short tuft of fluorescent hot pink yarn is tied over the top of the wing for added visibility.

Thorax: Pink sparkle dubbing
  - Kaufmann prefers Flame Stimulator SLF.

Thorax Hackle: Grizzly, slightly longer than abdomen hackle

How to Choose Elk Hair

Elk hair comes in many varieties, and even though the hair can vary from one animal to another or by where it comes from on a hide, there are some general guidelines to buying and using elk hair that will help your flies look and behave just right. Although elk hair is hollow like deer hair, neither hair is really hollow like a drinking straw. The hairs have a hard outer coating with a pithy, air-filled interior. Elk hair, in general, has a harder outer layer than deer, so it is less flexible and flares less, even though it holds almost as much air. As a result, elk is quite a bit more durable than deer hair.

Whether you are looking for deer or elk hair, look for hair that looks clean, straight, and even. Hair that curves to one side will make it tough to work with, as your wing will cock to one side or the other. Also look for hair with short, unbroken tips. All deer and elk hairs have thin black tips, but these tips are longer in some hair than others. Hair with long, flimsy black tips is difficult to even in a stacker, it is less durable, and it just gives the finished fly a sloppy look.

Bull elk, often called "light elk," is relatively short, blunt, and coarse, with pale cream tips. It offers just a slight amount of flare when pressure is applied with the fly-tying thread, and it is more durable than any other kind of elk hair. In its natural state, because of the light tips, it is also more visible on the water. It is the hair most commonly used for the Elk Hair Caddis, Humpies, and imitations of the paler species of stone flies. Typically, the tiny black tips at the very end of bull elk hair are short.

Cow elk is often called "dark elk" by fly shops. The hair is longer, coarser, and flares more readily than bull elk. The tips are tan, but a darker shade than the tips of bull elk. Cow elk is better for smaller caddis imitations, small Humpies, and anytime you want a darker wing that flares slightly more than it would with bull elk. Cow elk is not as hard and durable as bull, but it compresses easier under tying thread, making it less bulky.

Calf or "yearling" elk hair is similar to cow elk and many tiers have trouble distinguishing the two. It is typically thinner and longer than cow elk, so it has a wide range of uses, from very large Stimulators to tiny Elk Hair Caddis flies. It is also more difficult to find in fly shops. Because it is finer than cow or bull, it compresses into a small point on the hook shank, but because you can put more hairs in the same place, you can get a full wing or Humpy overlay without cramping space on the hook. Calf elk also tends to have shorter black tips than bull or cow, giving finished wings a clean profile.

You may also see elk mane, hocks, and rump for sale in fly shops. All of these hairs have little to no flare, and are best for tails on large nymphs and dry flies because they are stiff and durable. Elk mane is very long, dark, and stiff, and makes great tails for dry flies. It can be used on any pattern that calls for moose mane as a substitute. Elk hock is similar in color but shorter and finer, so it is better for dark tails on smaller flies. Elk rump is very coarse and stiff but is a pale cream color, so it is used for light-colored tails on large flies. Because elk mane and rump are so strong, winding a dark hair from elk mane and a light hair from elk rump makes a strong and realistic banded nymph body.

■ Typical examples of elk hair. The bull elk at the bottom left is best for big flies where durability and visibility are paramount. The cow elk at the bottom right is best for darker wings on big flies, and wings and tails on smaller dry flies. The calf elk at the top is longer and finer, and is versatile for all dry flies, especially the smaller ones.

from an all-night tying session in the middle of winter in his study. It came from years of adding new materials and then putting flies to the test, with many prototypes banished to the bluegill box before the final version was ready for the rest of the world.

Besides imitating stone flies of all sizes and colors (this fly is tied in a wide variety of color combinations), Stimulators work well in sizes 12 through 16 during caddis hatches, and in the bigger sizes a Stimulator makes a decent grasshopper imitation. I think trout take Stimmies for moths that bumble into the river. I've found Stimulators very effective during hatches of the giant *Hexagenia* mayfly, and although to most eyes it looks nothing like a big mayfly with upright wings, it could be a credible facsimile of a mayfly emerging from its shuck at the surface. And in small brook-trout streams where the average fish would fit into a sardine can, I've found that fishing a size 10 Stimulator while other anglers are fishing a size 16 Adams often helps me sort through the small fish and rise the eight-inch monsters.

Kaufmann doesn't offer many dictums when giving tying directions for his fly, but aspects he stresses are that the wing should be wide and tall and the tail should flare. The high wing gives the fly an impression of bulk and movement, dries quickly, and is highly visible even in foamy pocket water. The short, flared tail keeps the butt of the fly riding high, especially critical with this fly because it is often used as the dry end of a dry-dropper rig, with a weighted nymph tied to a piece of tippet that is attached to the bend of the hook.

■ Besides doing a great job imitating stone flies and grasshoppers, the Stimulator is an excellent imitation of moths that frequently fall into trout streams.

1 ▪ Start the thread just behind the eye of the hook and wind back to the point where the curve of the hook begins to point sharply downward. Cut a moderate amount of long elk hair with relatively hollow hair at the base. Clean all the short hairs out of it and roll the bunch in your fingertips to remove any bias the hair may have to curve to one side or the other. Even the hair in a stacker. Tie it in, beginning with a couple of relatively loose turns, then take a half-dozen tighter turns as you move toward the eye.

2 ▪ Slide the fingers of your left hand along the shank toward the eye to keep the hair from flaring. Spiral the thread through the hair until you are just forward of the halfway point on the shank.

3 ▪ Secure the hair with a half-dozen tight turns of thread. It will flare all over the place, so just trim the ends close to the hook shank with several cuts. Spiral the thread back to the tail. Tie in a piece of fine gold wire and wind forward to the halfway point.

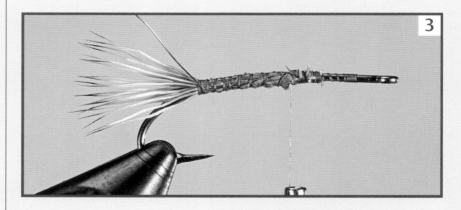

4 ▪ Select a brown saddle hackle with fibers about the same length as the gape of the hook or just a touch longer. Stroke a small portion of the fibers at the base until they are at 90-degree angles to the stem and trim them close. Tie in the hackle, dull side up. Leave a short portion of trimmed stem showing to give yourself some maneuvering room when you start your first turn of hackle. Wrap the thread back to the tail.

5 ▪ Dub a relatively thin body of orange sparkle dubbing. The body of the finished fly should have some bulk, but the elk hair underneath the abdomen will give it all the bulk it needs. Wind the dubbing forward to the point where you tied the hackle in.

6 ▪ Grab the saddle hackle with your fingers if it's long enough, or with hackle pliers if the hackle is too short to wind with your fingers. Wind it in close spirals back to the tail, shiny side facing forward. When you get to the tail, carefully switch hands and hold the hackle with your other hand. Wind the wire tightly over the last turn of hackle to secure it. Then, wind the wire forward over the hackle winds, wiggling it slightly to prevent binding down any hackle. Tie off the wire with the thread and trim it with a pair of scissors. Trim the tip of the hackle at the bend of the hook.

7 ▪ Cut a bunch of elk hair in the same manner as the tail. This bunch should be twice as thick as the tail bunch. Tie it in at the point where the abdomen ends so that it extends to about the middle of the tail with about eight tight turns of thread. Let the hair flare so that it forms a distinct but loose bunch that extends over the top 180 degrees of the hook.

8 ▪ Advance the thread forward into the butt ends of the wing. Make tight turns and let the hair flare all over the place, binding it in tightly. Don't stop until all the butt ends have been bound down and don't worry about being neat.

9 ■ Trim the butt ends of the wing with several cuts at various angles. Trim it close to the hook shank. Wind thread back and forth over the ends to bind them down. Bring the thread back to the base of the wing.

10 ■ Select a grizzly saddle hackle or long neck hackle with fibers just a touch longer than the body hackle, about one-and-a-half hook gapes in length. Stroke a small portion of the fibers at the base until they are at 90-degree angles to the stem and trim them close to the stem. Tie in the hackle, winding forward, dull side up. Leave a short portion of trimmed stem showing to give yourself some maneuvering room when you start your first turn of hackle.

11 ■ Advance the thread to just behind the eye. Dub a thin length of reddish orange sparkle dubbing. Not only will you be making a double layer of dubbing here, you also already have substantial bulk on the hook shank, so don't overdo it.

12 ■ Wind the dubbing back to the base of the wing, then forward to just behind the eye. Add a small amount or remove some dubbing if you don't have quite the right amount.

13 ■ Wind the grizzly hackle forward through the thorax in tight turns, dull side forward. Tie off the grizzly hackle just behind the head.

14 ■ Whip finish and add two drops of deep-penetrating head cement to the bare thread winds.

The Humpy is really a style of dry fly and not a single pattern, although when someone says the word "Humpy" fly fishers invariably think of its most popular color variation, the yellow one. The Humpy evolved from earlier western deer-hair dry flies, beginning with the Horner Deer Hair, originated by San Francisco fly tier Jack Horner in the 1930s and often called the "Little Jack Horner." Although Horner may have been the first tier to construct a dry fly with a hump of hair pulled over the body of the fly, his original pattern was designed more to sit in the film than to float high in fast water, as he called for only four turns of hackle. A modern Humpy typically has about 12 turns of hackle and is a much bushier fly. Horner also did not use colored bodies on his flies, but merely crisscrossed the hair under the hump with black tying thread.

Later, tiers in both Montana and Idaho added heavier hackle, divided the hair wings (Horner used only a single upright clump of blacktail deer hair for his wing), and added different colored threads for the underbodies. Pat Barnes began selling this new variation, which he obtained from a Montana guide named Keith Kenyon, in his western Montana fly shop in the 1940s, calling it the Goofus Bug. In the same decade, Leonard "Boots" Allen of Wyoming was tying and selling a similar pattern he called the Humpy. Even today in Montana you might hear people call this fly a Goofus Bug, but it's the Wyoming name that really stuck.

In the 1970s, Jackson Hole fly tier, author, and fly-shop owner Jack Dennis developed the Royal Humpy variation by cutting off the tips of the elk hair and adding upright wings of white calf tail for greater visibility. He also began tying his standard Humpies with elk hair, a variation that is considered standard in fly tying today. Elk hair was a big improvement in Humpy construction. It is less difficult to handle than deer hair because the coarser elk stacks and cleans easier; elk hair is far more durable than the finer deer hair; and elk is a paler cream than the dull gray of deer hair so it is easier to see the fly in fast water.

The Humpy is an all-purpose fly that is deadly not only on tumbling Rocky Mountain rivers, but also anywhere trout eat insects. It is as popular on transparent New Zealand trout pools as it is in the pocket water of Chilean coastal rivers. The Humpy is one of the most effective small-stream flies for New England and the Smoky Mountains of the Southeast, and I have tied it as small as a size 24 for spring-creek trout eating midges. I have no idea what the trout think it is. Maybe in smaller sizes it looks like a midge pupa emerging at the surface or a leafhopper struggling in the surface film. All I can be sure of is that this particular combination of materials appeals to trout whenever they are inclined to look at the surface for food.

Pattern Description

Hook
Standard dry fly, sizes 10–18, or Bigeye hook in smaller sizes

Thread and Body
Yellow 6/0

Tail
Elk mane or the tips of fine cow elk hair

Wing and Body Overlay
Large bunch of long, coarse, hollow elk hair from a calf or bull elk

Hackle
Brown and grizzly
Long, narrow, domestic saddles are best, but long neck hackles can also be used.

Pattern Variations

GREEN HUMPY

Hook: Standard dry fly or Bigeye hook in smaller sizes

Thread and Body: Bright green 6/0

Tail: Elk mane or the tips of fine cow elk

Wing and Body Overlay: Large bunch of long, coarse, hollow elk hair from a calf or bull elk

Hackle: Brown
- Long, narrow, domestic saddles are best, but long neck hackles can also be used.

ORANGE HUMPY

Hook: Standard dry fly or Bigeye hook in smaller sizes

Thread and Body: Fluorescent fire orange 6/0

Tail: Elk mane or the tips of fine cow elk

Wing and Body Overlay: Large bunch of long, coarse, hollow elk hair from a calf or bull elk

Hackle: Brown
- Long, narrow, domestic saddles are best, but long neck hackles can also be used.

*Note: See also **Royal Humpy** in the variations for the Royal Wulff (page 69).*

Hackles for Big Dry Flies

Hackles for dry flies have come a long way in the past 30 years, thanks to pioneers like Buck Metz, Tom Whiting, Henry Hoffman, and Bill Keough. Prior to the development, through genetics research and lots of trial and error, chicken hackles for dry flies came from India, where the chickens were free-range raised for food. Vast quantities of rooster and hen hackle capes were skinned and bundled for shipment to fly-tying suppliers in the United States and United Kingdom, where they were fumigated (by law), sorted by color, graded, and packaged. Indian hackles were short but stiff, and were fine for standard dry flies, but when a tier wanted to tie a Wulff or Humpy with bushy hackle, it may have taken three or even four feathers to give the fly enough hackle.

Indian saddle hackles were usually not stiff or glossy enough; they had fibers that were too long for standard dry flies and had too much web. There were a few small, secretive operations in the United States producing chicken hackles just for fly tying—by individuals like Harry Darbee or Andy Miner—but to get one of these capes you really had to know someone who knew them and even then the cost of a hackle cape would be almost as much as a production-grade bamboo rod.

In the 1970s, larger-scale operations for growing fly-tying hackle began producing what we now know as "domestic hackle." Feathers became longer and finer, and instead of needing two or three hackles to tie one fly, tiers were faced with the dilemma of a single hackle feather that would tie three flies! Unfortunately, the idea of a hackle cape with an abundance of tiny size 18–26 hackles became a symbol of quality, even though most tiers want hackles in sizes 12–16. But luckily, at the same time, the neck capes were improving and saddle hackles from farther down the neck of the chicken were making huge strides in quality as well; it is now possible to find saddle hackles that will tie dry flies from size 10 down to size 20. Because saddles typically grow hackles suitable for a range of only two or three sizes, today dry-fly saddles are often sold by size, either on the skin or in packages, and some of these hackles can easily tie four or five flies.

If you tie a wide variety of sizes, a neck hackle cape is probably your best bet, as they have the widest range of sizes. However, if you tie a lot of Humpies and Wulffs (and other large dry flies) in sizes bigger than a number 14, you'll eventually want some saddle hackles. With the emphasis in premium hackle capes on the smaller feathers, the large feathers at the top of the cape tend to be poor quality with thick stems, which make for sparse, messy dry flies. Saddle hackles are easier to wind in the bigger sizes and do not exhibit the thick stems common in large neck hackles.

One final advantage of using long saddle hackles is the ability to wind two hackles at once with your fingers. It's tough to wind two hackles together with a pair of hackle pliers, as one hackle invariably slips from the pliers' grasp as you wind. But the longer saddles allow plenty of working room for your fingers, and with more precise fingertip pressure, you have more control over where the hackle winds fall.

■ Three very different kinds of hackle capes, each with a size 14 hackle taken from the neck to its left. On the left is an Indian hackle cape, with short hackle length and few hackles smaller than size 18. In the middle is a domestic hackle cape grown for fly tying, with long hackles and a wide variety of sizes. On the right is a half-saddle cape (just a saddle cape split in half) that will only offer hackles in two sizes, but the length allows the tier to tie at least four flies from a single feather.

1 ■ Start the thread in the middle of the hook shank and wrap back smoothly to the normal tail tie-in point. Snip a small amount of fine calf elk hair from the hide and even the ends in a narrow stacker. Measure the tails against the shank and tie them in so they are just slightly shorter than the shank. Avoid putting too much tension on the first wrap or two to keep the tails from flaring. Wrap forward smoothly over the elk hair to the middle of the hook shank, increasing tension as you move forward.

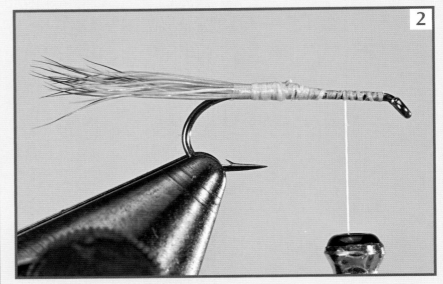

2 ■ Trim the ends of the elk hair as close to the hook as possible. Wrap forward to the eye and then back to a point about one-quarter of the way toward the bend of the hook. The few wraps forward to the eye help provide a base for later, when you wrap hackle, without creating a lot of bulk.

3 ■ Cut a relatively thick bunch of elk hair from a piece of bull elk with long hairs that are hollow at the base and have broad pointed tips. The exact thickness will depend on the size you are tying, but cut about 75 percent more than you think you will need because a lot of the small hairs and fuzz at the base will be removed. Make sure the hairs are at least two inches long so you have room to make the hump and to manipulate it easily when making the body. (It also helps if the hair is as long as possible; when it comes time to trim the ends of the hump, it's difficult to separate the hairs that you are trimming from the

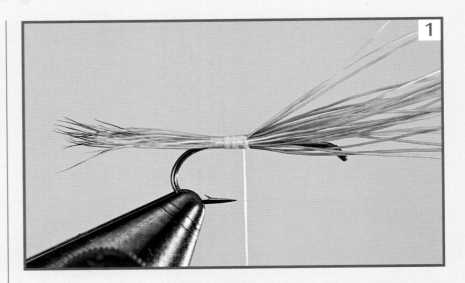

fibers of the wing, which you don't want to trim.) Hold the hair by the tips and remove all the short hairs and fuzz from the base. Make sure you remove any hairs that are less than three-quarters of the length of the longest hairs, as these will only get in the way when you try to make the body. Place the bunch in a wide stacker and even the ends.

4 ▪ Measure the tips of the elk hair against the shank and tie them in, pointing over the eye, so that the wings are equal to the length of the shank. Pinch the sides of the hook so the hair does not roll over the shank and tie it in place with about 10 very tight, closely spaced turns of thread. Work back slightly toward the bend with each subsequent wrap.

5 ▪ Grasp the bunch of elk hair and hold it at about a 45-degree angle above the hook shank. Spiral the thread back over the bunch, keeping it on top of the hook shank, until you are right above the tie-in point for the tails.

6 ▪ While you continue to hold the bunch of elk hair above the hook, wrap thread back and forth over the hook shank, until you have all traces of the hair wrapped under and you have a smooth yellow underbody. Leave a gap just behind the wings as shown so you don't have as much bulk where you will be tying off the body and tying in your hackles.

7 ■ Wind the thread to a point just behind the wings, leaving a gap for the base of the hackle winds. Keeping the elk hair above the shank, pull it forward over the wings. Make sure you separate this bunch from the tails carefully before you pull it over the top. Take a single loose turn of thread over the elk hair and then tighten very firmly with a straight downward pull. Take three or four more turns of thread in the same way. Make sure you pull up slightly on the elk hair as you bind it in to keep it on top of the body.

8 ■ Carefully pull up the thicker, blunt hairs that made the overlay for the body. Separate them from the finer hairs that will become the wing by pulling them straight up in a single bunch. Trim these hairs very close to the hook shank, making a couple of cuts if necessary. It's a good idea to put a drop or two of deep-penetrating or thinned head cement on the butt ends of these hairs as the point where they are tied in is the weakest part of a Humpy tied in this manner.

9 ■ Wind a smooth base for the hackle behind the wings. Use a lot of tension so that this area does not get too bulky—the base of the hairs will compress as you wind over them tightly. Bring the thread in front of the wing and wind thread until the wings stand upright on their own. Elk hair does not need as much thread in front to hold it upright as deer hair or calf tail does.

10 ▪ Separate the wing into two equal bunches with a dubbing needle. Make a single figure-eight wrap by winding between the wings on top from front to back while holding onto the near wing, under the hook shank, and then between the wings from back to front while holding onto the far wing.

11 ▪ Take two turns of thread around the base of the far wing. Wind one turn around the shank and then take two turns of thread around the base of the near wing. Bring the thread around in back of the wings.

12 ■ Sort through a bunch of brown and grizzly saddle hackles with fibers that are between one-and-a-half and twice the length of the hook gape. Find one brown and one grizzly with fibers that are exactly the same length by stroking about 10 to 12 fibers at the very base of the feather down toward the base until they stand at right angles to the stem. Overlap the feathers to make sure they match. Trim off the fibers that you just stroked out very close to the stem. By leaving these little nubs, your hackle will not pull out as you wind it.

13 ■ Tie in both hackles at the same time, with dull sides facing up and the butt ends passing between the wings. One or two of the nubs closest to the tip of the hackle should not be tied under so the hackle gets a good start in the right direction before the fibers begin to flare around the hook. If the stems extend beyond the front of the wings, carefully snip them off.

14 ■ Bring the thread forward to a point just shy of the eye. Grab both hackle fibers together and begin winding them forward. With most feathers, you will get two turns behind the wing and two turns in front. Make sure that the last turn behind is very close to the base of the wings, and the first turn in front is right up against them, so that when you jump in front of the wings you will not be leaving a gap in the hackle and the hackle fibers will stay at right angles to the hook and not slant forward or backward.

15 ■ Once the hackle is just shy of the eye, hold both hackles close to the fly on top of the hook shank. Pass the thread over both hackles and secure with three very tight turns, pulling straight down. Trim the ends of the hackles very close to the hook shank and wind another six tight turns over the stub ends.

16 ■ Push the winds just behind the eye back slightly with the nails of your thumbnail and forefinger. Grasp all the hackle, pull it back slightly, and make two additional winds up against the last turn of hackle—don't wind over the hackle, just up against it.

17 ■ Neaten the head with a couple more turns of thread if needed. Whip finish and apply a drop of deep-penetrating head cement to the bare thread winds at the head.

Nymphs

Frank Sawyer spent most of his life, from 1928 through his death in 1980, as river-keeper of the River Avon in England. He became intimate with the trout and insects of this spring-fed, productive river with lush weed beds, and his familiarity with the entire ecosystem convinced him that artificial nymphs, fished upstream to fish he could spot in the clear water of the Avon, were the most productive flies. He experimented with a number of very simple but effective fly designs, flies that could be tied in a few minutes, yet were the ultimate in refinement. His most famous fly was the Pheasant Tail nymph, which gained worldwide acceptance in the second half of the 20th century in trout streams and lakes around the world.

The Pheasant Tail was developed by Sawyer to imitate the larva of various species of olive mayflies. The genus *Baetis* in particular is the most abundant mayfly type in the world, occurring in nearly every trout stream in both the northern and southern hemispheres, thus the universal appeal of Sawyer's fly. It's amazing that an artificial fly with shades of brown and orange is so successful for the brownish-olive nymphs of the *Baetis* genus, and Sawyer himself was mildly perplexed at the discrepancy in color. He discusses this in his book *Nymphs and the Trout*:

> Though I give full credit to fish in being able to differentiate between general colours and sizes, I am quite sure that in the brief time they have in between seeing, and taking an artificial, it is not possible for them to see a mixture of several different materials.

Pattern Description

Hook
2XL nymph hook, sizes 12–18

Thread
Brown or orange, 6/0 or 8/0

Weighting Wire
Lead, tin, or copper wire

Tail
Pheasant tail fibers from a center cock pheasant tail

Rib
Copper wire

Abdomen
Pheasant tail fibers from a center cock pheasant tail

Wing Case
Pheasant tail fibers from a center cock pheasant tail

Thorax
Peacock herl, three strands from the bottom of a large peacock eye

Legs
Pheasant tail fibers from a center cock pheasant tail

What is more I came to the conclusion many years ago that they see colours in a different way than we do ourselves. This is of course impossible to prove. The red of the pheasant tail body and wire tying that I use could not possibly be mistaken by us for an olive, or greenish yellow colouring. Yet fish take it readily when creatures of this latter colouring are hatching.

He gave great credit to the tiny fibers for adding movement and translucency, and observed how the pheasant tail material held tiny bubbles to give further credence to the impression of a live insect. And because he was trying to imitate a swimming mayfly that tucked its legs under its body when swimming, he left legs off the pattern entirely. Leaving legs off the fly also gives it less resistance in the water and makes it sink quicker without much added weight.

Sawyer tied the Pheasant Tail nymph in a distinctive manner that is the epitome of efficiency, and once you learn his technique, finished flies can be cranked out in just a few minutes—or even less time in the hands of a professional tier. The Pheasant Tail was tied with only two materials plus a hook—a single bunch of pheasant tail fibers and copper wire. First, he would wind a very fine copper wire onto the hook shank, building up the thorax area with several layers of wire for weight and to get a tapered shape. He then tied in the ends of the pheasant tail bunch for the tails of the natural with two or three turns of wire. Leaving the wire hanging at the tail, he wound the fibers forward almost to the eye. He then ribbed the wire through the pheasant tail, binding it down just behind the eye. Next, he spiraled back quickly to the back of the thorax, folded the pheasant tail over for a wing case, spiraled the thread back again to the eye, and folded the pheasant tail over the thorax a second time. By using just the right length of pheasant tail, by the time he reached the folded wing case, the darker roots of the pheasant tail formed the perfect dark, humped thorax of a *Baetis* nymph. The result is an elegant and deceptively simple fly.

The Pheasant Tail emigrated to North America, where it became popular on our spring creeks, which resemble the English chalk streams. Famous fly tier Al Troth of Dillon, Montana, liked the Pheasant Tail, but felt it did not have enough bulk or the profile of many of our faster-water mayflies, with their wide thoraxes and more prominent legs, which are often splayed to the sides when drifting instead of tucked under as in the slimmer swim-

BEADHEAD PHEASANT TAIL

Hook: 2XL nymph hook, sizes 12–18

Thread: Brown or orange, 6/0 or 8/0

Tail: Pheasant tail fibers from a center cock pheasant tail

Rib: Copper wire

Abdomen: Pheasant tail fibers from a center cock pheasant tail

Wing Case: Pheasant tail fibers from a center cock pheasant tail

Thorax: Brass or tungsten bead, copper color

Legs: Pheasant tail fibers from a center cock pheasant tail

ORIGINAL FRANK SAWYER PHEASANT TAIL

Hook: 2XL nymph hook, sizes 12–22

Thread: Fine copper wire

Tail: Pheasant tail fibers from a center cock pheasant tail

Rib: Fine copper wire

Abdomen: Pheasant tail fibers from a center cock pheasant tail

Wing Case: Pheasant tail fibers from a center cock pheasant tail

Thorax: Pheasant tail fibers from a center cock pheasant tail

Note: Sawyer used only a single bunch of pheasant tail fibers to construct the entire fly, but if the fibers on a tail aren't long enough, different bunches can be tied in for each part of the fly. The fly is often tied commercially with standard tying thread in orange to match the copper color of the original tying material.

ming mayflies so common on chalk streams. He made a variation of the fly with prominent legs and a bulkier thorax to better imitate the nymphs he was seeing, still keeping the basic essence of that magical pheasant tail material. But now there were two Pheasant Tail nymphs swimming in American waters, creating confusion. Troth's fly was tied weighted with lead wire and with standard thread, and its profile was really quite different from the Sawyer Pheasant Tail, so it was truly a new pattern. Thus the name Troth Pheasant Tail, or American Pheasant Tail, to distinguish the two.

The American Pheasant Tail is now tied in scores of variations, with flashy material pulled over the top of the fly and metal beads on the thorax to create the Flashback Pheasant Tail. The beaded version is by far the most popular style today, with its flashy thorax and weight that help trout pick it out in fast, turbulent water. But there is still a place for the slimmer, Sawyer-style Pheasant Tail on spring creeks, tailwater rivers, and lakes, especially when small olive mayflies are hatching. I carry plenty of both styles in my fly box.

Working with Beads

Beadhead nymphs and streamers took the world by storm in the 1980s. Originally used in Austria, the first beadhead flies were imitations of caddis pupae and utilized solid brass beads with small holes in the center, in contrast to the brass beads seen on light chains, which were hollow but with much thinner walls and not as much weight. Once anglers saw how effective the beadhead flies were, with the ability to sink a nymph without adding weight to the leader—although many nymph anglers now use both beadhead flies and weight on the leader for fast, deep water—they began to add beads to all manner of nymphs and streamers. Some patterns with double bead dressings were developed, especially for large stone flies.

The brass (or gold) color was followed by copper, silver, black, and fluorescent colors. Fluorescent colors are typically used on steelhead flies, and the question of whether to use a silver, gold, or brass bead on a nymph or streamer is totally up to the tier's aesthetic sense or a guess as to which version is more appealing to the fish. For instance, on a Pheasant Tail nymph the common bead to add is a copper one, to match the ribbing color and overall coloration of the fly. And the Prince nymph has a gold rib, so it makes sense to add a gold bead to that pattern. Adding a bead to a fly may or may not make it a new pattern, depending on your fly-tying philosophy, but all of the popular nymphs now have beadhead variations.

For a while it looked like some states were going to ban lead in all fishing tackle, including flies, and there was an especially serious talk of a lead ban in California and Yellowstone National Park. Because brass has a small amount of lead in it, I worked with a friend, Ron Kurtz, who then owned a tungsten manufacturing company, to develop a tungsten bead, and it turned out the beads were almost twice as heavy as the equivalent brass bead. You can now buy tungsten beads in the same colors as brass beads, but they are more expensive.

One color that is not used as often as it probably should be is the black version. In heavily fished waters, I'm quite sure that fish caught and released numerous times get wary of any piece of food with a big flash at its front end, and on some rivers, beadhead flies don't get the same response that they used to receive. Under these circumstances, I've found that nymphs with black beads are far more productive, especially if the bead is buried under dubbing or other materials. Why use a bead at all if you're going to hide it? Because I think that beads, especially tungsten beads, are a very efficient way to add weight to a fly, and adding a tungsten bead gives a nymph about twice the weight of adding an underbody of tin wire, which most tiers use now in place of toxic lead.

When turning a nymph into a beadhead version, tiers usually just leave off the fur or peacock herl of the thorax and substitute a bead for this part of the fly, pulling the wing case material over the bead. Beads should be slipped onto the hook prior to beginning the fly. Some beads are difficult to slip over the bend of the hook, but a handy trick is to grab one side of the bead with a pair of forceps, which aids in slipping the bead around a difficult bend. There is a narrow and a wide end of the hole in the center of a fly-tying bead, and the narrow end should face the eye of the hook so it does not slip off the front end. The bead is usually placed just behind the eye of the hook, and should be glued in place with Super Glue or head cement. Otherwise, the bead could slip back over the rear of the fly. It also helps to build up thread or materials on the rear side of the bead for added security.

■ If you have difficulty getting a bead around the bend of certain hooks, guide the bead with a pair of forceps as shown.

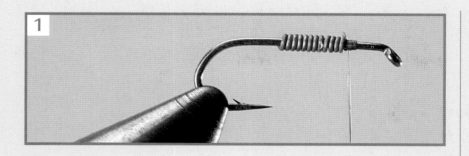

1 ■ Wind the center of the hook with weighting wire. Start the thread in front of the wire while you hold the rear in place with a fingernail. Spiral back quickly over the wire and build up a bump of thread behind it to hold it in place. Apply a few drops of head cement to the wire to keep the finished fly from rolling around the hook.

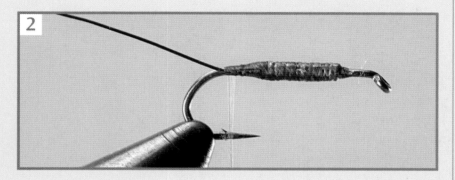

2 ■ Immediately behind the underbody wire, tie in a piece of copper wire for the rib. Wind over this wire back to the beginning of the bend, then wrap the tying thread back and forth over the rear of the body to form a tapered underbody.

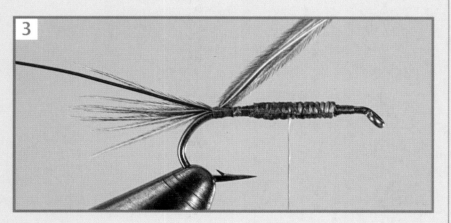

3 ■ Return the thread to the bend. Snip eight to 10 pheasant tail fibers from a large center tail feather from a cock ringneck pheasant. It helps to align the tips of the fibers before snipping them. Tie in the pheasant tail fibers with four very tight turns of thread, so that the tips extend about three-quarters of a hook-shank length beyond the bend, but don't bind down the butt ends. Bring the thread forward to the middle of the body.

4 ■ Wind the pheasant tail forward in non-overlapping turns. Tie off in the middle of the body with about six tight turns of thread.

5 ■ Wind the copper wire through the body in even spirals. Tie off the copper wire in the same place as the pheasant tail fibers. Some people wind the wire in a direction at a right angle to the spirals of the pheasant tail for added durability. Although it may not be quite as durable, I like the looks of winding the wire at the same angle as the feather fibers.

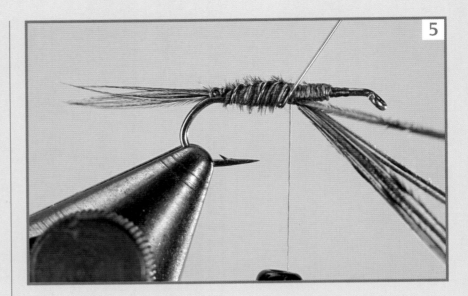

6 ■ Cut another eight to 10 pheasant tail fibers in the same way you did the tails. Measure them so that the place where you pinch your fingers when you tie them in is one hook-shank length down from their tips. Tie these fibers in at the middle of the hook with the tips pointing back toward the bend. Wind forward a half-dozen turns to bind them in, trim the butt ends, and wind back to the middle of the hook shank again.

7 ■ Cut three pieces of peacock herl from the bottom of a large tail feather. Trim the tips so they are even and tie the herls in by their tips, just in front of the pheasant tail fibers. Wind forward over the tips of the herl and trim them, leaving a small space behind the eye.

8 ▪ Wind the herls forward to just behind the eye. Tie off with four very tight turns of thread. Trim the ends close to the hook shank.

9 ▪ Bring the pheasant tail forward over the peacock herl and tie it in just in front of the herl tie-off point.

10 ▪ Separate the ends of the pheasant tail into two equal bunches. Pull them back along the sides of the thorax and wind back over them for a few turns, until they lie in place along both sides of the thorax. Finish off with a small, smooth head, whip finish, and add a drop of head cement to the bare winds.

Caddis pupae are among the most difficult insects to match when trout are feeding on them. When caddis pupae are emerging, the angler must have the correct combination of both imitation and presentation, and it's one instance where trout—opportunistic feeders under most circumstances—just don't give you any leeway. Get one part of the puzzle wrong and you're in for a day of frustration. If you do happen to get it right one day and it seems like you can't keep trout off your hook, don't get too arrogant. The next time you encounter trout eating the same bugs, the solution you thought was universal may not lead to success.

Gary LaFontaine, of Deer Lodge, Montana, was one researcher who got as far as anyone in developing a reliable, effective imitation of caddis pupae. In concert with a small army of entomologists and fly fishermen, he spent 10 years writing a book and developing his fly patterns. The 1981 book *Caddisflies* was met with a mixture of elation and skepticism because LaFontaine had claimed to crack the code on caddis pupa imitations—elation because trout anglers everywhere were constantly frustrated when fish ate caddis pupae; skepticism because his fly patterns were not only unorthodox, but they also incorporated a

Gary LaFontaine

Pattern Description

new material, Antron yarn, about which he made bold claims.

LaFontaine observed that there are two major periods of hesitation by the insect during any emergence. The first is when the pupae emerge from their larval cases and hesitate near the bottom while they develop gas bubbles under their exoskeletons. The second is when the pupae try to break through the surface of the water. Contrary to popular belief, which states that caddis flies rocket through the surface film and take off, LaFontaine determined that the meniscus presents a tough barrier to the emerging insect because of the strong bonding properties of water in contact with the air. He likened it to a human trying to push through three feet of dirt.

These two periods of hesitation by the insect were when trout fed most heavily on caddis pupae. LaFontaine developed two similar flies to imitate them—the Deep Sparkle Pupa to imitate the hesitation near the bottom, and the Emergent Sparkle Pupa for the insect pushing through the meniscus. The Deep Pupa was tied on a nymph hook and incorporated lead or copper wire in the body to keep the fly near the bottom; the Emergent Pupa was tied on a dry-fly hook, and although the body was the same as the Deep Pupa, it added an emergent wing of hollow deer hair to keep it pinioned in the surface film.

It was known that caddis pupae were covered with air bubbles when emerging, but imitating that sparkle with metallic tinsel or other body materials

■ A caddis pupa, that annoying little bug that trout love and whose imitation Gary LaFontaine spent so much time developing.

Pattern Variations

DARK GRAY DEEP SPARKLE PUPA

Hook: Standard or 2XL nymph hook, sizes 10–18

Thread: Match body color, 6/0 or 8/0

Underbody: A mixture of one-half dark brown fur and one-half gray sparkle yarn

Overbody: Gray Antron

Legs: Gray hen hackle, sparse and tied along the lower half of the sides

Head: A few brown marabou strands or brown fur

Note: All of LaFontaine's patterns can be tied in any color variation. This is just one variation on the Brown and Bright Green pattern.

EMERGENT SPARKLE PUPA
(Bright Green Color Variation)

Hook: Standard dry fly, sizes 10–18

Thread: Match body color, 8/0

Underbody: A mixture of one-half bright green synthetic dubbing fur and one-half olive sparkle yarn

Overbody: Olive Antron
  - Fibers from the top portion are left trailing in the back to imitate the pupa shuck.

Legs: Fine deer hair, sparse

Head: A few brown marabou strands or brown fur

of the day were unsuccessful. Then LaFontaine discovered DuPont Antron, a flat-sided, trilobal fiber that not only reflected light in the same way as air bubbles, but also attracted and held air bubbles. The yarn was developed as a stain-resistant, non-matting fiber for carpets, and the sparkle of the fibers helped mask the presence of dirt and stain in a rug. It was the solution LaFontaine had been looking for in his pupa imitations.

It's doubtful that any trout fly was ever as exhaustively researched as LaFontaine's pupa imita-tions. Besides the 10 years he spent talking to fish-ermen and entomologists, testing imitations, and working with DuPont to discover the secrets of Antron yarn, LaFontaine also spent 211 hours underwater watching caddis pupae emerge and trout react to the insects. By reading his book you would think he was a bizarre mad scientist, but in person he was warm, generous, and centered. The fly-fish-ing world lost one of its brightest stars when Gary LaFontaine died in 2002 at the age of 56 after a long battle with Lou Gehrig's disease.

Antron, Z-Lon, and LaFontaine's Sparkle Yarn

The original material Gary LaFontaine used for his Sparkle Pupa patterns was a soft yarn with very fine fibers, and the yarn consisted of a mixture of clear and colored Antron fibers. The yarn is no longer made, but the business LaFontaine established, The Book Mailer of Helena, Montana, contracted to have a run of the material made and still sells it. In contrast, the fly-tying material sold in most fly shops as Antron yarn today is a uniformly dyed color and the fibers are larger in diameter. Yet a third fiber also used interchangeably is Z-Lon fiber.

All of these fibers are trilobal; in other words, if you looked at a single fiber in cross section under a high-powered microscope, it would be triangular with flat sides. These flat sides provide a more reflective surface and are not as likely to mat together when wet because of the physical properties of the shape. In addition, the trilobal shape helps the fibers hold air bubbles, which is important to help create the impression of the shimmering profile of an emerging caddis pupa.

If you look at all three fibers side-by-side, there are minor differences. LaFontaine's original yarn offers more of a subtle sparkle because of the clear fibers incorporated into the yarn, and because of its finer fibers, it has a fuzzy look. Antron yarn sold on spools today is more translucent overall because of the heavier fibers, but it has a straighter texture that makes it more difficult to develop a soft halo effect on the shuck of an imitation. It's easy to kink this yarn slightly to get a better shuck by pulling it tightly through your fingernails until it frays. Z-Lon is processed to retain a naturally kinky nature, which makes it more resistant to matting. It holds even more air bubbles, and is effective for both overlays on caddis pupae and shucks on emerging mayfly and caddis fly imitations.

All three fibers seem to make a positive difference in effectiveness when tying emerger patterns, and it's worth having at least one on your tying desk, as ordinary yarns don't create the same effect.

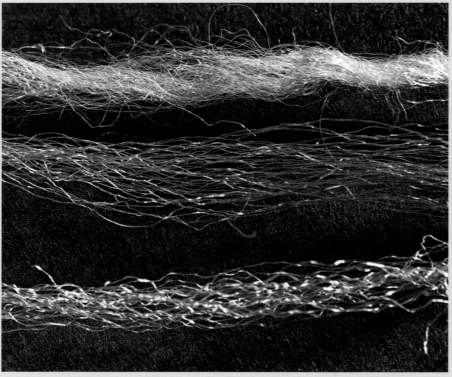

■ Materials used for shucks and overlays in caddis pupae and emergers. On the top is a strand of the original Antron yarn used by Gary LaFontaine, with a mixture of clear and dyed fibers. In the middle is dyed spooled Antron, the type available in most fly shops. On the bottom is Z-Lon yarn, which has more of a distinct kink.

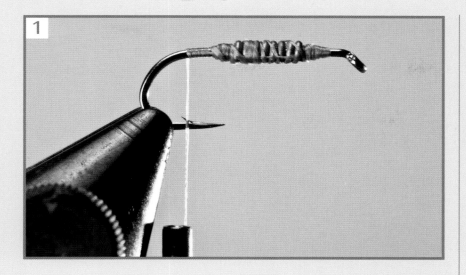

1 ▪ Wrap wire, either nontoxic or copper, over the middle half of the hook. Start the thread in front of the wire weight. While keeping the rear of the wire in place with your thumbnail, wind thread in front of the wire until a small bump is wrapped tight to the wire. Spiral the thread quickly back to the rear of the wire and make a similar tight bump behind it to keep the wire in place. Wrap thread back and forth over the wire a few times to further secure it.

2 ▪ Separate the three strands of a piece of sparkle yarn if you are using three-ply yarn; if not, separate a single strand of Antron yarn so that you have about a two-inch piece. Using a fine wire brush or flea comb, brush the yarn until the strands are separated and fuzzed up slightly. Brush hard enough to separate the fibers from each other, but not hard enough to remove strands from the piece. Cut this piece in the middle so that you have two even ends to tie in. Tie one strand on top of the hook, pointing back beyond the bend of the hook, binding down the ends until they meet the end of the wire so you get a smooth layer to dub over.

3 ▪ Turn the hook over in the vise. Tie the other strand on the underside of the hook in the same way. This lower overbody strand won't encircle the lower half of the hook properly unless you turn the hook upside down in the vise and tie it in pointing backward so that it straddles the hook.

4 ▪ Dub the thread with the underbody and wind forward to a point that is about one-quarter of the way back from the eye. Pick or brush out the dubbing slightly to give it a fuzzy look. The best tool I have found for this is a very fine copper wire brush.

5 ▪ Pull the top strand loosely over the back of the fly and tie it in just ahead of the body with two loose wraps of thread. Turn the fly over and do the same with the bottom strand. Don't trim the ends yet.

6 ▪ With the tip of your dubbing needle, gently lift each strand separately. Then, with your thumbnail and dubbing needle, distribute the overbody until it encircles the hook.

7 ■ Now, take several tight wraps of thread forward away from the body to secure the ends of the overbody. Trim the ends of the overbody just behind the eye.

8 ■ Tie in a few strands of partridge or grouse on each side of the head. Place the strands alongside the body where you want them, wrap the thread loosely over them once, and then apply gentle pressure to the thread toward the opposite side of the hook.

9 ■ Take about five strands of marabou and trim the fine ends so you have an even tie-in spot. The fluffier marabou fibers from the base of a feather work best. Tie in the marabou by the fine ends on top of the hook shank, right up against the body. At this point, make sure the area between the marabou and the eye of the hook is smooth and does not have any bumps or slopes in it. Otherwise, the head will be difficult to get right. Wind the marabou forward two or three turns and tie off.

10 ■ Stroke the marabou back slightly, form a short, neat head behind the eye, and whip finish. A drop of deep-penetrating head cement applied carefully to the whip finish will seep back into the base of the delicate marabou and help strengthen it. Don't worry if some of the fibers of the underbody or overbody trail back behind the fly. Many tiers leave a few trailing on purpose to imitate the trailing shuck of the natural pupa.

12 Prince

The three most popular nymphs in use in North America today are the Prince nymph, the Hare's Ear nymph, and the Pheasant Tail nymph. All of these flies have nearly endless variations: they are tied with brass or tungsten beads in several colors, with standard or flashy wing cases, with synthetic as well as natural materials. If you looked at fly popularity west of the Mississippi River, the Prince in its many variations would edge out the other two—although it is no slouch on eastern trout streams either. It seems that every fly tier who stumbles upon a slight variation of the Prince nymph calls it a new pattern. Based on what I have discovered about Doug Prince, the originator of this pattern, he'd be happy with the outcome, as he tied many variations of what we call the Prince nymph, and it's only one of the many variations that was named after him.

The Prince, like many effective trout flies, is an enigma. No one has ever seen an insect with white horns crossed over the top of its body, although it's possible they may imitate the wing pads of a mayfly or stone fly larva once they have filled with gas bubbles in preparation for hatching. This theory makes sense when you examine one of the most popular modern variations of the fly, a pattern named The Fly Formerly Known as Prince, a name that elicits a chuckle, especially from anglers who were teenagers in the 1990s. The fly substitutes pieces of flashy pearlescent tinsel for the white biots and is especially popular with fishing guides in the Rocky Mountains.

■ The Prince Nymph is even more popular today as a beadhead version.

Pattern Description

Hook
2XL nymph hook, sizes 8–18

Thread
Black 6/0

Tail
Two brown goose biots

Rib
Flat gold tinsel (oval is often used as well)

Body
Peacock herl

Wing
Two white goose biots tied flat over the back

Hackle
Brown hen hackle

Another popular variation, used for both trout and steelhead, is the Dark Lord, created by California guide Ron Hart in the 1980s. It's a deadly pattern when small dark stone flies are active, so it makes an especially good winter nymph when stone flies are the most common insect active on trout streams.

Most fly fishers use the Prince as a stone fly imitation, and it seems to be especially effective in rivers with dense stone fly populations. The stiff, forked tails certainly mimic the robust tails of a stone

Doug Prince, unlike tiers today, tied his biot wings curving upward; somewhere along the way it became acceptable to tie them curving down. These two were tied by the author from descriptions of original Doug Prince ties (as described to him by Randall Kaufmann).

fly larva. However, given the effectiveness of the Prince at nearly any time of year, it's possible that fish mistake the fly for a swimming mayfly larva or even a larval fish. But it's really not worth agonizing over—the Prince is an effective subsurface pattern when you're not sure what trout are feeding on, and is as often recommended in the mountains of Chile and New Zealand as it is in the Rockies.

What we do know about originator Doug Prince is that he worked in the insurance business in Los Angeles and frequently made the drive north to fish the Kings River outside of Fresno, California. The Kings River is a relatively large, tumbling tailwater river that has had ups and downs over the years, but in the middle of the 20th century it was one of the premier trout streams in California. The noted fly tier Ed Schroeder, who developed such effective trout flies as the Hare's Ear Parachute and Parachute Hopper, grew up fishing the Kings River and has a vivid memory of his first meeting with Prince:

I was fishing the Kings in 1964, just a snot-nosed kid who really didn't know much about fly fishing for trout. I was stumbling around one day when I came upon a woman sketching on the bank who I later learned was Doug's wife. She asked me how I was doing and with a kid's directness I answered, "Not good." Doug was out in the river fishing, and when he heard me he waded back to the bank and introduced himself. He was pretty well-known in those days, but of course the name meant nothing to me. Doug told me to hold out my hand and he proceeded to dump at least two dozen flies in my hand, most of them what we'd now call the Prince nymph. He then spent the whole day fishing with me, teaching me how to fish nymphs. You just don't find that kind of person on trout streams today. You're lucky even to get a greeting out of most people now.

Prince was probably the first tier on the West Coast to use biot fibers (the stiff, short fibers on the leading edge of the primary wing feathers, typically from a goose but they can be found on any primary feather), but he was not the first one to use them for nymph tails and wing pads. He first saw the progenitor of his pattern tied by brothers Don and Dick Olson of Bemidji, Minnesota. The Olsons tied a fly they called the Brown Fork Tail, which, besides the biot tails and wing pads, used black ostrich herl for the body. Also of note is that both the Olsons and Prince tied their biot wings with the concave side of the feather facing up, not cupped to the body as we tie the Prince nymph today.

Legendary fly tier Randall Kaufmann fished and tied with Doug Prince in the 1970s, and his most treasured fly collection is a set of 20 of Prince's favorite flies, framed in a shadow box. Looking at these flies today, Randall describes the ones closest to what we call the Prince nymph:

> Doug tied the Prince several ways, but the black ostrich and the peacock were his favorites. One Prince is tied with peacock and oval gold rope rib and another Prince with black ostrich and oval silver rope rib. The wing or horn biots (both white) curve upward. The tail biots curve outward, forming a V, black on the black, white on the peacock. The peacock version has a full circle sparse brown hackle. The black has three-quarter underside black hackle. These were referred to early on as the Brown Forked Tail and Black Forked Tail.

It seems that Prince retailed the original names he learned from the Olson brothers and never claimed to have originated the style of tying used on the Prince nymph. The name was likely appended to the fly in honor of Prince, who was a generous friend to all anglers. How the fly gradually mutated to its current form is unknown, but we now accept that either oval or flat tinsel is OK and that the fly should be tied with the wing horns curving downward—although it might pay to experiment with Prince's original profile.

Pattern Variations

DARK LORD

Hook: 2XL nymph hook, sizes 8–18
Thread: Black 6/0
Bead: Black or brass
Tail: Two brown goose biots
Rib: Oval gold tinsel
Body: Black fur dubbing
Wing: Two amber goose biots tied flat over the back
Hackle: Black hen hackle

THE FLY FORMERLY KNOWN AS PRINCE

Hook: 2XL nymph hook, sizes 8–18
Thread: Red 6/0
Bead: Gold
Tail: Two brown goose biots, splayed using the red tying thread
Rib: Flat gold tinsel
Body: Peacock herl
Wing: Two pieces of pearlescent holographic film or tinsel trimmed to the shape of biots
Hackle: Brown hen hackle

Wet Fly and Nymph Hackle

Chicken hackles are often used on wet flies and nymphs, and many tiers just use lower-quality dry-fly rooster hackle (shorter feathers and those with too much web at the base) for the hackle on wets. This is economical, but not always practical given the state of the hackle market today. The dry-fly hackle we use is so good that there is very little waste on a hackle cape or saddle, and the only place on most hackle feathers you can find web is at the very base of the feather, if at all.

Hen hackles are much better for wet flies and nymphs for a number of reasons. First, they're inexpensive. Where a prime quality dry-fly cape sells for around $70, you'd be hard-pressed to pay any more than $20 for the best hen cape you can find. Second, hen hackles always have finer stems than rooster hackles, which makes tying and folding the hackle easier and the resulting fly has less bulk at that critical area in the front of the fly where most materials get crammed. And third, hen hackle is softer and more flexible, so it moves and breathes with every little current, suggesting the tiny movements of insect legs better than stiffer rooster hackle.

It's easier to fold wet-fly hackle and give it that elegant swept-back look by tying it in by the tip. Hackles tied in by the butt always want to slant forward, where feathers tied in by the tip sweep back toward the bend of the hook with little coaxing. To do this easily, stroke the fibers of the feather down toward the base (again, it's much easier to do this with hen hackle than rooster hackle) and carefully snip the fibers at the tip of the feather close to the stem. By tying in this stubby tip, the thread grabs all the tiny fibers next to the stem and your hackle is less likely to slip out in the tying process or after the fly is completed. Once the hackle tip is tied in place, stroke all the fibers back toward the bend of the hook until they all appear to originate on the back side of the feather. Make one turn of hackle and then stroke the fibers again so they continue to flow backward. Hackle on most nymphs and wet flies should be sparse, so two or three turns is usually all it takes.

 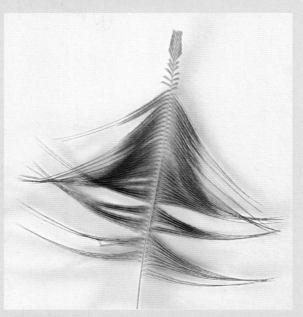

▪ **Left:** Hen hackle, on the left, has a finer stem and fibers with more webbing, so the hackle moves with every little current and produces a much more lifelike nymph or wet fly. Rooster hackle, on the right, has a thicker stem and stiffer fibers. **Right:** Hen hackle prepared for tying. The fibers are stroked down from the tip and the fibers at the very tip of the feather are trimmed.

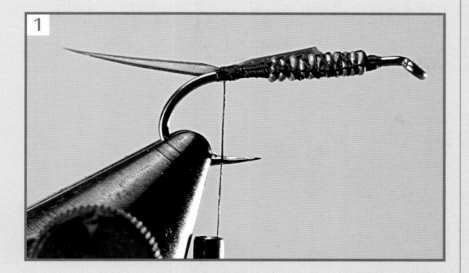

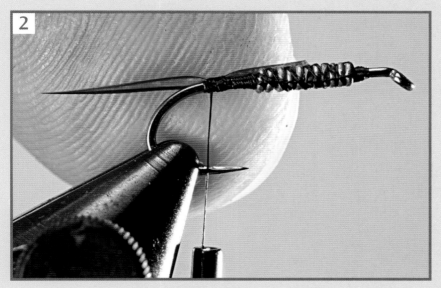

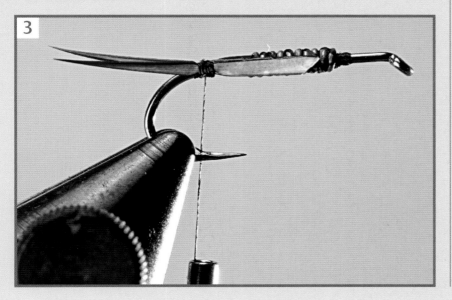

1 ▪ The Prince, if not tied with a beadhead, is most often tied weighted, so wind about half the shank with weighting wire, leaving plenty of room at the front and back. Attach black thread to the hook just behind the eye and while you hold the rear of the lead wire in place with your fingernail, wind a small bump of thread in front of the wire. Spiral the thread back quickly to the tail and wind another bump of thread behind the wire. Wind the thread back and forth over the wire several more times to further secure it. Cut two brown goose biots from close to the tip of the feather, as the tails should be thinner than the wings and biots are thinner toward the tip of the feather. Measure one biot against the shank. The tails should stick out beyond the bend about one-half of the shank length. Hold this biot against the far side of the hook.

2 ▪ Take one relatively loose turn of thread around the biot while holding it against the far side of the shank with your forefinger. Then take a couple of tighter turns, pulling the thread straight up when you tighten to help place it against the shank without rolling over the far side.

3 ▪ Take the second brown biot and lay it against the near side of the shank until it is equal in length to the first biot. Take one loose turn of thread to place it, and then several more, pulling the thread straight down when you tighten to help hold it against the side of the shank. When properly placed, the tails should splay outward from each other. Hold both tails against the hook with your thumb and forefinger and wrap the thread forward to just behind the end of the wire. Trim the biots just flush with the end of the wire.

4 ■ Tie in a piece of flat gold tinsel just behind the wire. If it is the older metallic-style tinsel with gold on both sides it doesn't matter which side of the tinsel faces the hook shank, but most likely you will be using more modern plastic tinsel with gold on one side and silver on the other. Make sure the flat gold face of the tinsel is tied facing away from you, against the hook shank, so that the silver side is showing. Wrap the tinsel smoothly back to the base of the tails on the near side of the hook shank, and finish up with the tinsel on the near bottom of the hook shank.

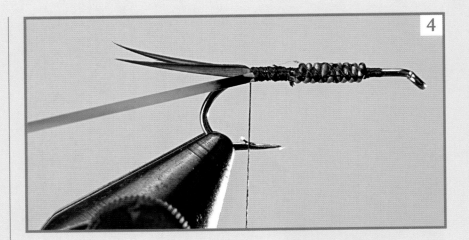

5 ■ For the larger size 8 and 10 nymphs, find about five adjacent peacock herls from just below the eye that don't have broken ends or any gaps in the herl fibers. For smaller flies, use three or four herls farther down the eye so that the flue—the tiny fibers along the herl—is not as long. This way you won't end up with a fly that is too fat on the smaller versions. Line these herls up so the tips are relatively even before you cut them from the stem, then cut them all together so the tips are perfectly even. Cut the herls just below the tips so the finer ends are all lined up and easier to tie in neatly, and tie the herls in at the base of the tail and wind forward to the end of the weighting wire. Trim the ends just shy of the wire and then wrap the thread back and forth until you have built up a smooth taper from the tail to the wire. (The original Prince nymph used a black rabbit dubbing underbody, but most tiers today use weighting wire wrapped with black thread for the same effect with less effort.)

6 ▢ Wind the herl forward to a point about one-eighth to one-sixteenth of the hook-shank length back from the eye of the hook. By tying in the herl by the tips, the entire flue should flow backward as you wind it so that none of the fibers get bound under by preceding turns. Tie in the herl on top of the hook shank with several very tight turns of thread. Trim the herl as close to the hook shank as possible.

7 ▢ Wind the tinsel forward in a spiral, ensuring that it has flipped over on the first wind so the gold side is facing out. Turns should be spaced so that enough herl shows between succeeding turns to give the body a full profile. On most flies, you'll take about four or five evenly spaced turns. Tie in the tinsel at the same spot as the peacock herl, but underneath the hook shank.

8 ▢ Select a brown hen hackle with fibers that, when held up against the shank of the hook just behind the eye, extend about three-quarters of the way back to the point of the hook. Stroke the fibers down from the tip of the feather toward its base. Trim the very tip of the feather, cutting fibers from each side almost to the stem for a short length just below the tip of the feather. The little nubs along the stem will help hold the hackle in place when you tie it in. Tie in this trimmed section.

9 ▢ Hold the hackle above the hook and stroke the fibers on the feather back toward the bend of the hook so they all point back on one side of the stem. Wind two or three turns of hackle, stroking the fibers back after each turn so they all flow back toward the point of the hook.

10 ■ Split the hackle fibers on the top of the hook with your fingers. Pull the hackle fibers back toward the bend and under the hook, then hold them in place with your thumb and forefinger and wrap three turns of thread back over them, angling the thread so that it wraps back slightly over the tops of the hackle winds on top of the hook. When you finish, the hackle should be nicely distributed around the bottom half of the hook. Wrap a smooth base of thread to hold the wings with a layer or two of thread.

11 ■ Trim two white goose biots from the base of the feather where the biots are shorter and wider. Measure one biot so that it extends to the point where the tails begin. Tie it on top of the hook shank, pointing just slightly away from you, with the concave side of the biot facing down.

12 ■ The best way to tie on the biot is to angle the butt end toward you just a bit, place your forefinger on top of the biot to hold it in place, and take two or three turns of thread to secure it. Don't trim the butt ends yet.

13 Take the second white biot and tie it in the exact same place, with the butt end angling just slightly away from you. Examine the wings from the top of the hook. They should be symmetrical and form a narrow V-shape over the top of the body. If one is cocked too much in either direction, move the butt of the biot slightly to move it into place. When you are satisfied that they look correct, make a few tight turns over the butt ends, keeping one forefinger on top of the hook to keep them in place. Now trim the butt ends of both biots.

14 Wrap a neat head over the material that is still showing forward of the winds, whip finish, and apply a small drop of high-gloss head cement.

15 This is the finished fly, showing the proper position of the wings from the top.

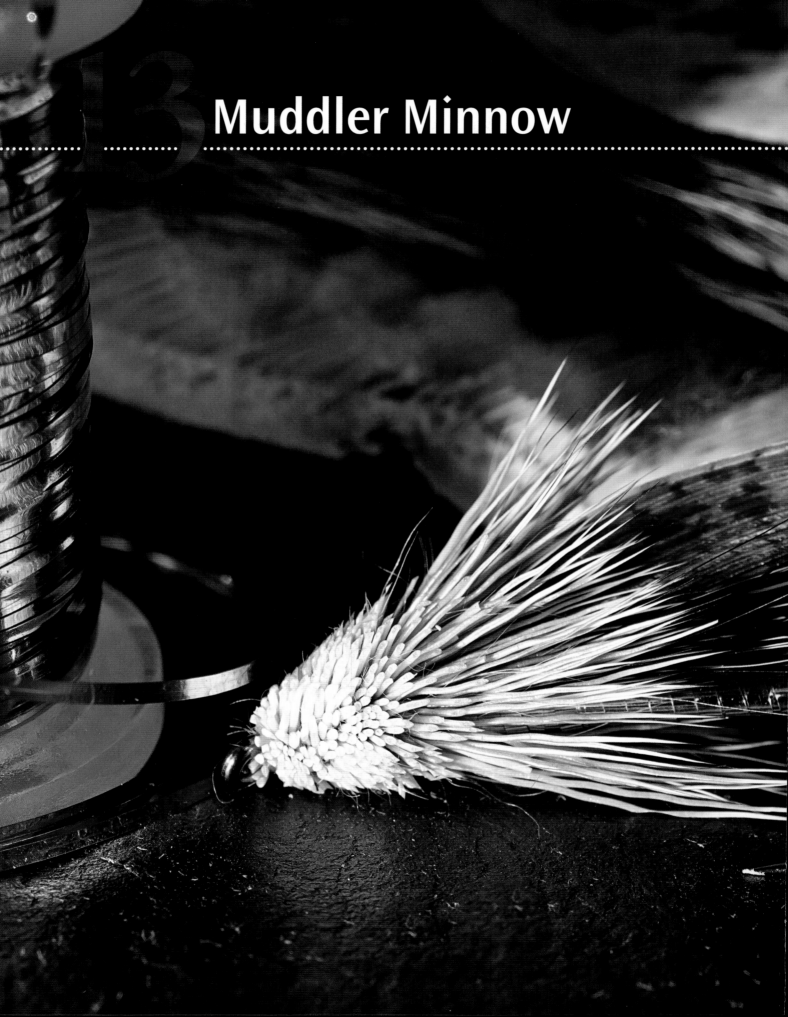

13

Muddler Minnow

Prior to the popularization of the Woolly Bugger, the Muddler Minnow probably accounted for more large trout caught on a fly in the 20th century than any other pattern. As with any fly pattern, its popularity is part marketing hype, part visual appeal, and part effectiveness, but the original Muddler has no sex appeal—it's a drab, fuzzy creature that, when introduced to the public in the 1940s, looked nothing like the sleek, colorful streamer fly patterns that originated in Maine. So, in this case, we have to credit pure effectiveness as the reason for the Muddler's fame.

The pattern was originated in 1937 by lodge owner and guide Don Gapen on the Nipigon River in Ontario, Canada. The world-record brook trout was caught on this river earlier in the century, and in the 1930s, it was still a popular destination for those anglers looking for a giant brookie. Gapen noticed that the local Ojibwa Indians used a small bottom-dwelling baitfish they called a cockatush, which was known in Minnesota—where Gapen was from—as a muddler. In most of North America this fish is known as a sculpin, and it is one of the favorite prey of large trout and bass.

There is some dispute as to exactly how Gapen tied his first Muddlers. Some sources claim that the original pattern had no tail and a simple wing with a turkey feather over a bunch of wolf hair; they also claim that the wolf hair at the front was trimmed to imitate the broad, flattened head of a sculpin. Others claim that the pattern had a deer-hair head from the very beginning. In a photograph from the collection of Ted Patlen of an original Muddler tied by

Pattern Description

Hook
4X long streamer, sizes 2–12

Thread
Tan and white 3/0

Tail
Slip of mottled turkey quill

Body
Flat gold tinsel

Underwing
Gray squirrel tail

Wing
Pair of mottled turkey wing quills

Collar
Deer body hair tips

Head
Spun and trimmed deer hair using the butt ends of the collar combined with a second bunch of deer body hair

Gapen, the head is definitely made from deer hair, but it is unknown whether this photo is a Muddler from its first years or after later variations. What is very apparent is that although we still tie the Muddler Minnow from the same materials that Gapen used, the silhouette of the fly has changed dramatically.

The most noticeable difference is that Gapen's deer-hair heads were bigger and sparser. If they were trimmed at all they were trimmed very roughly, which actually makes more sense when trying to imitate a sculpin, as these fish live close to the bottom. Today's tightly spun deer-hair heads keep the fly more buoyant than the loose arrangement favored by Gapen. When we tie the fly today, we use a fairly sparse bunch of squirrel tail for the underwing, overlaid by large

slips from a mottled turkey wing. Gapen's flies were the opposite—a large, bushy hunk of squirrel tail flanked by narrow slips of turkey. Also, the deer-hair collar on Gapen's flies was much longer and sparser than the short, stacked bundles of deer hair we use today to imitate the large pectoral fins of the sculpin.

Dan Bailey of Livingston, Montana, was responsible for the fly's popularity in the American Rockies, and through his friendship with Joe Brooks, who traveled the world for the 1960s TV series *The American Sportsman*, the fly was introduced to fly fishers from Australia to Argentina. It was probably due to Bailey's influence as a commercial fly tier that the Muddler got its tightly spun and neatly trimmed head, as a fly with a neater appearance sells better in the fly bins. Bailey also originated perhaps the Muddler's best and most popular variation, the Marabou Muddler. Bailey tied the Marabou Muddler in a variety of colors, but the most popular today are white, yellow, and black.

Although its resemblance to the mottled brown color and flattened shape of a sculpin accounts for some of the Muddler's effectiveness, the fly has appeal far beyond just a baitfish imitation. Gapen and others noticed that when greased with fly floatant, the fly makes a superb dry grasshopper imitation. When fished dry, it

■ An original Gapen Muddler, from the Ted Patlen collection and photographed by T.C. Geist. Note the rough, sparse head and large amount of squirrel tail flanked by narrow slips of turkey.

Pattern Variations

WHITE MARABOU MUDDLER

Hook: 4X long streamer, sizes 2–12

Thread: White 3/0

Tail: Two red hackle tips

Body: Silver tinsel chenille

Wing: White marabou plume

Topping: A few strands of peacock herl

Collar: Deer body hair tips

Head: Spun and trimmed deer hair using the butt ends of the collar combined with a second bunch of deer body hair

YELLOW CONEHEAD MARABOU MUDDLER

Hook: 4X long streamer, sizes 2–12

Thread: Tan or yellow 3/0

Tail: Two red hackle tips

Body: Flat gold tinsel or gold braided tinsel

Wing: Yellow marabou plume

Topping: A few strands of peacock herl

Collar: Deer body hair tips, with the butt ends trimmed to meet the rear edge of the cone

Head: Gold colored brass or tungsten cone

Note: The cone is placed on the hook before tying the fly and secured with Super Glue or epoxy. No extra bunch of deer hair is needed after the collar is tied in, and the butt ends of the collar are flared and then trimmed to meet the cone. This pattern can be tied in any color (the most popular are white and black), and a cone can also be added to a standard Muddler.

also has a passing resemblance to a large stone fly. Fished under the surface, dead drift, the Muddler is perhaps the best imitation of a drowned grasshopper in most people's fly boxes, and although most anglers fish it either with strips as a streamer or dry as a grasshopper, wary trout feed more readily on drowned grasshoppers than live floating ones. Adding a couple of split shot to the leader ahead of a Muddler Minnow is often a way to take trout during grasshopper season when the fish don't seem inclined to come to the surface.

When fishing a Muddler Minnow as a streamer, it's best to weight the fly because the tightly packed deer-hair heads we use today are so buoyant. Probably the best way to add heavy weight to a Muddler is to tie a conehead version, especially using a tungsten cone, which is much heavier than brass. The Muddler can also be tied with heavy wire under the tinsel. Tying flat tinsel over a wire underbody makes an ugly fly, however, so if lead or nontoxic wire is used as weighting, it's best to make the body out of gold diamond braid, tinsel chenille, or even

Spinning Deer Hair for Muddler Heads

As with most flies, obtaining the right material is key to getting a finished fly that looks like the original, or at least like the ones you see in a fly catalog. Deer hair used for Muddler heads (and for most trout fly deer-hair spinning) should be coarse and straight, with blunt tips that don't end in long black hairs. Coarse hair spins better, as it is hollower, floats better, and is more durable. An added benefit is that part of the appeal of flies with Muddler heads may be that the rough texture of the head sets up vibrations in the water that are felt by a fish's lateral line, even in the dark or in dirty water. The coarser the hair, the more bubbles and turbulence the head will make. Blunt tips without curvature are much easier to use in forming a neat collar, as hair that curves to one side or another will roll around in a stacker and come out sticking in all directions, rather than as a neat bundle. (Of course, a collar that sticks out in all directions could actually be more appealing to fish, so this note is merely for those who want to tie flies that elicit bragging rights from fellow fly tiers.)

For spinning, avoid hair that is too fine or that has a kink in it, and look for lighter-colored

Essential items for nice deer-hair heads: a pair of sharp, serrated scissors or a double-edged razor blade, and a piece of deer hair with coarse, round fibers and short, blunt tips.

natural hair, which will have shorter black tips. Good spinning hair is not necessarily long, either. Some of my best spinning hair is just over an inch long, but has short blunt tips and a coarse, round texture, which is easier to find on the shorter hairs from the flanks than on the longer hairs from the back or belly of a deer.

When spinning hair, make sure you use thread that can put a lot of pressure on a large bunch of deer hair without breaking. Most sources recommend size 3/0 or G thread for deer hair. However, it should also be as fine as you can get away with, because really heavy thread won't bury itself into the head and may show up after being trimmed (or even worse, you could cut the thread in the process of trimming). When tying a small Muddler with sparse bunches of hair, however, size 6/0 may be acceptable if you can put enough pressure on the hair so that the thread really digs into the hair and binds it to the shank.

The best way to trim a Muddler head is with a double-edged razor blade. Carefully break the blade in half with two pairs of pliers and use one side at a time. You can make your cuts with the blade straight and keep going around the edges to round it, or you can carefully bend the blade between your thumb and forefinger to get a curved shape that will give you a cone-shaped head with fewer cuts. Don't be thrifty with these blades, either. They're pretty cheap if you buy them in bulk. I find that after two flies a blade does not cut as cleanly as it did and I'm ready to use a fresh one.

Muddler heads can also be cut with a pair of scissors, but it's not as fun and is more work than using a razor blade. If you do use scissors, make sure they are sharp and serrated. Without tiny serrations on one blade, even the sharpest scissors will slip off some of the hairs instead of cutting them cleanly, and you'll end up with a Muddler that looks like one of Don Gapen's originals!

gold Mylar tubing, all of which tie much neater over a weighted body. Of course, the Muddler can also be fished with a sinking or sink-tip line, but even with a sinking line the fly tends to ride toward the surface because the head holds so much air.

It's important to get matched mottled turkey wings to tie a Muddler. If the wings are not properly matched left and right wing quills, the stiffness and curvature of the two sides won't match and the wings will slant to one side no matter how precisely you tie them in. For the wings on this fly, the feather sections should be taken from the short side of the wing feather, where the curvature is constant and coloration is usually better. The long side of the feather on the opposite side of the stem is usually straighter and wings set from this side usually won't cup into each other properly, although this lack of curvature does make a good

tail, where typically only a single feather (rather than a matched pair) is used.

The Muddler can be tied with the wings curving upward, with concave side down, or with concave side up. Most tiers put the concave side down so that the wing makes a nice arc across the back of the fly, imitating the prominent dorsal fin of a sculpin. Heads can also be trimmed to any shape desired. The classic Muddler head (as least as we know it today) is conical when viewed from the front and is good as a general-purpose fly that can be used as a streamer today and a dry grasshopper imitation tomorrow. However, some tiers trim the head to a flatter shape that is wider than it is tall, which better imitates the broad head of a sculpin. And, of course, if you are interested in historical accuracy, you can always spin the head loosely and trim it roughly or not at all.

■ The original Muddler Minnow imitates the blunt head, wide pectoral fins, and banded body of a sculpin, a very important baitfish for large trout.

1 ■ Attach white thread to the hook about one-third of the distance from the eye and wind back to the bend. Try to keep the area behind the eye free of thread and materials. Cut a slip of feather from mottled turkey wing. This can be from the long or short side of the wing quill, but as it is a single piece, you'll want it to be without much curvature. By taking a piece from the long side, you are more likely to have a curve in the feather. Place the feather over the tie-in point at the end of the hook. It should extend slightly more than the length of one hook gape beyond the bend. Take a loose turn over the feather, then pinch it in between your thumb and forefinger and tighten firmly with a straight downward pull of the thread. Take two more tight turns and begin to wind forward. Make sure the subsequent turns do not wind back over the feather or it may collapse or cock off to one side.

2 ■ Continue to bind the feather under, winding forward with smooth, tight turns of thread, avoiding lumps or gaps. The feather will try to slide around the far side of the hook, but try to keep it on top or cupped over the top of the hook shank with equal amounts of material on each side. Otherwise, the tinsel body will appear lumpy. Trim the feather at a point just shy of where you began the thread.

3 ■ Tie in a piece of Mylar tinsel with two turns of thread. The short end of the tinsel should be pointing toward you and the gold side should be on top. Do not trim the short end of the tinsel.

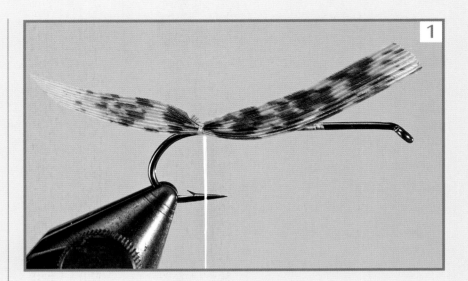

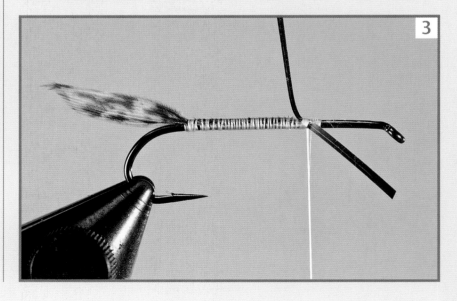

4 ▪ Begin winding the tinsel toward the rear with wraps that just slightly overlap the previous ones. Keep pressure on the tinsel to make it dig into itself slightly. When you get to the tail, hold onto it and cover the remaining turn of thread, then begin to wind back toward the eye. Don't wind over the tail or you might move it out of alignment. It is tough to see the second wrap of tinsel as it goes forward over the previous wrap; adjust your light so that you can see the wraps and make sure each is smooth and overlaps the preceding one slightly.

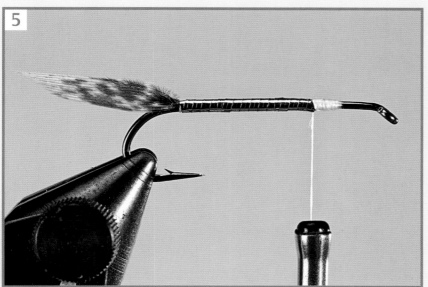

5 ▪ Tie off the tinsel where the tag end was left. Use about four tight turns of thread. Now, trim both ends of the tinsel as close to the hook as possible. Wind forward a few turns to provide a base for the squirrel tails, and wind back to the end of the tinsel body.

6 ▪ Cut a bunch of gray squirrel tail about as wide as the gape of the hook. Clean the short hairs and fuzz from the bunch. Don't even think about trying to even it in a stacker—squirrel tail doesn't stack well and this fly should not have that evened-off look anyway. Place the squirrel tail on top of the hook and tie it in with a pinch wrap and four or five tight turns of thread.

7 ▪ Trimming the ends of squirrel tail is difficult because the stuff is, well, squirrely. Hold the wing firmly when you lift and trim the butt ends so that it won't roll around the hook. Cut the ends off on a slight taper, keeping the area behind the eye free to spin the deer-hair head, and then wrap over the ends while holding the wing in place.

8 ▪ From a matched pair of turkey wings, snip a section from the left and right side at about the same point on the wing feather so the curvature matches. They should be about twice as wide as the tail at their widest points. Place the left wing against the far side of the squirrel tail so that it extends almost to the end and is pointed up slightly. The feather should hug the far side of the hook just at the tie-in point. Take the matching feather section and place it on the near side so it matches the length and attitude of the far wing. I find it easiest to wet the tip of my finger and pick up the feather section that way. Slide the near side forward or back until it matches the length of the feather on the far side.

9 ▪ Take a loose turn of thread over the wing, pinch it against the tie-in point, and tighten the thread with a straight downward pull. Take about four or five more tight turns, moving slightly forward with each turn. Keep pinching the wing so it stays in place.

10 ▪ Carefully trim the butt ends of the wing with a pair of sharp scissors. Try not to move the butt ends too much as you snip them to avoid moving the wing. Wrap thread smoothly over the wing butt, whip finish, and add a drop or two of head cement over the bare thread winds. Put this assembly aside for 15 minutes to dry. This might be a good time to tie another wing/body assembly.

11 ▪ Attach tan thread to the spot where the wing assembly was finished off. Clean all the fuzz and short hairs out of a bunch of coarse deer hair—about as big in diameter as the gape of the hook—and even it in a stacker. Place the deer hair on the far side of the hook so that the tips extend to about the middle of the wing. Take one loose turn of thread around the bunch, then a second tighter turn, and then two or three very tight wraps, holding the deer hair in place so that it covers just the far side of the hook. The thread should bury itself in the hair and disappear; if it does not, you have not used enough tension. Don't let go of the hair, and allow it to spin all the way around the hook.

12 ▪ Add a second bunch of hair, the same diameter and length, to the near side of the hook in the same manner. At this point, deer hair should encircle the whole hook; if it does not, move it around a bit with your thumbnail. Take a few very tight wraps forward until the thread is in front of the deer hair. With your thumbnail or a hair packer, push the hair back until it stands upright, then take several more tight turns right in front of the hair.

13 ■ Cut a third bunch of deer hair—as large as the hair on both sides of the wing combined—and clean out the fuzz and short hairs. This time, trim off the tips so the bunch of hair is blunt on both ends and no more than three-quarters of an inch long. This will make it spin easier. Tie this hair in over the bare portion of the hook shank, leaving a small gap in front to finish the head. Take one loose turn of thread, a second slightly tighter turn so the hair begins to spin, then a third very tight turn. Let go of the hair and let it spin completely around the hook. Make four or five very tight turns to further spin and secure the hair. Bring the thread in front of the hair, pack it backward with your thumbnail, and wind enough of a head in front of the hair to keep it pointing straight up and not over the eye.

14 ■ Whip finish by holding all the hair back with one hand and manipulating the whip finisher with the other. Be careful not to catch any hairs when you whip finish. With one side of a double-edged razor blade, make initial cuts all the way around the head at about a 30-degree angle. Don't cut all the way back to the collar yet.

15 ■ Pull any long, blunt hairs that are still mixed with the collar forward and trim these from around the collar with a pair of sharp scissors. Finally, go back around the head with the razor blade a second time to give it a final shape.

16 ■ Add a drop of deep-penetrating head cement to the head and tip the fly back so the cement seeps back into the hair winds.

14

Woolly Bugger

The first time I saw a Woolly Bugger in action, the fly did something I had never seen before. I was fishing on the upper Beaverkill in New York State with bamboo rod maker Ron Kusse, who at the time was running the Leonard Rod Company and was trying to convince me—a young kid fresh out of college with a fisheries degree and who could tie flies but had no other visible skills—to run his new retail store. It was an achingly bright, sunny afternoon, the kind of day that means long, boring dry spells between fish. We were sitting on the bank, watching nothing but current flowing by, and he stood up and said, "Watch this." Kusse cast to the far bank and stripped something through the pool. In the middle of the barren-looking pool, where it seemed like you could see every rock on the bottom, three trout chased his fly across the water, practically cart-wheeling across the surface. None of them connected, but on the second cast a trout smacked the fly and then released it.

"What the hell kind of fly are you using?" I asked. He replied that it was called a Woolly Bugger, and Barry Beck had recently showed it to him. When I got a look at the fly, I realized it was nothing more than a Woolly Worm, an ancient wet fly, with a long marabou tail. I was disappointed in the fly's simplicity, but was intrigued by its effect on the fish. That was 1976, and in a few years the Woolly Bugger had spread around the world—even

Russell Blessing

Pattern Description

Hook
4X long streamer, sizes 2–12

Thread
Black 3/0

Tail
One or two bunches of black marabou

Body
Olive chenille

Hackle
Black hackle palmered through the body

without the boost it would have received via the Internet years later—proving that sometimes just adding one simple ingredient to a standard fly pattern can pull it ahead of the pack with a vengeance.

For years I thought Barry Beck had developed the fly (although he never claimed to), but I later learned that Beck got the fly from his fishing buddy, Russell Blessing, a modest man who, despite creating the deadliest fly since the Muddler Minnow, never asked for any recognition. I finally convinced Beck to tell me the story, as Russell Blessing unfortunately passed on just as I was beginning this book. "Russ had no ego," Beck told me. "Although he was a very good fisherman, he never wanted any credit for the fly, said it was just an accident and he was happy that so many people were successful with it."

Beck met Blessing during a Trico hatch on the Little Lehigh River in Pennsylvania in the late 1960s. After the hatch, when the action quieted down, Blessing was catching fish one after another and Beck finally asked him what he was using. Blessing showed the fly to Beck, and admitted he just put a marabou tail on a Woolly Worm. He first tied the fly in 1967 as a dobsonfly imitation for smallmouth bass, and when fishing for smallmouths (and trout), he often put a single split shot

just above his clinch knot to get the fly to kick and look like a jig. Beck was so impressed with the fly that he wrote about it for *Fly Fisherman Magazine* in the early 1980s. "At the time I was also tying flies commercially," Beck told me. "My first order from Orvis was for 150 dozen Woolly Buggers, the largest order I had ever gotten from them."

The Woolly Bugger has spawned hundreds of variations since, and it seems as though every angler has his or her own variation of a fly with a marabou tail, palmered hackle, and a chenille or yarn body. I've seen (and used) Woolly Buggers in purple and pink for steelhead, chartreuse for striped bass, tan for bonefish, yellow for largemouth bass, and, of course, many different shades of both neutral and bright colors for trout and smallmouth bass. Flashabou or similar material can also be added to the tail for more sparkle when fishing fast, deep, or dirty water, although I find at times a muted color palette is more effective, especially for smallmouth and trout. I'm sure there are very few fish that will take a fly that have not been caught on a Woolly Bugger, from pumpkinseed sunfish to tarpon.

Everyone knows how to tie a Woolly Bugger; it's typically the first fly anglers learn to tie. So on this one, I thought I would stay true to the original pattern, still the most popular, and give you a couple of tying tricks that will make yours better. One will keep it from fouling when you have a tailwind or your loops are too tight; the other will make your flies neater and more durable and was shown to me by my son when he was four years old. The foul guard is a simple loop of monofilament that is often used on tarpon flies, when you may have only a few shots at a fish per day and you don't want the tail of your fly to foul around the hook bend when you make that important cast. I frequently find that my Woolly Buggers foul, so I thought adding this feature to the fly would be a natural variation.

The other trick, taught to me by my son, Brett, was a revelation. He had a fly-tying bench next to mine and often worked on his own creations

CRYSTAL BUGGER

Hook: 4X long streamer, sizes 2–12

Thread: Black 3/0

Tail: One or two bunches of black marabou

Body: Olive Crystal Midge yarn or similar sparkly material

Hackle: Black hackle palmered through the body

BLACK TUNGHEAD WOOLLY BUGGER

Hook: 4X long streamer, sizes 2–12

Thread: Black 3/0

Tail: One or two bunches of black marabou

Body: Black

Hackle: Black hackle palmered through the body

Head: Black tungsten or brass cone

EGG-SUCKING LEECH

Hook: 4X long streamer, sizes 2–12

Thread: Hot orange 3/0

Tail: One or two bunches of black marabou

Body: Black

Hackle: Black hackle palmered through the body

Head: Two wraps of fluorescent pink, fluorescent orange, fluorescent red, or chartreuse chenille

while I was distracted with tying. I taught him to strip the fuzz from the core of a piece of chenille while tying it in and I happened to glance over at him while he was tying. I noticed that he was also stripping the fuzz from the other end of the chenille before tying off at the head. Why didn't I ever think of that? It secures the bulky chenille without building up a big mound at the head when you tie it in.

I think all buggers need at least a small amount of weight because the marabou tail and palmered hackle make the fly pretty buoyant. Even when fishing at night or in small streams with a Woolly Bugger—where you want your fly

to run relatively shallow—I still add some heavy wire to the underbody to get it below the surface. If you want to fish a Woolly Bugger in deeper pools and fast runs without resorting to a sinking line, put a tungsten bead or cone at the head before tying the fly, or tie in lead hourglass eyes like those used on the Clouser Minnow.

Saddle hackle behaves better than neck hackle for this pattern. It's much easier to wind and has nice, uniform fibers, which gives the fly a nice look and action in the water. I like saddle hackle that is about half web so that the fibers wiggle in the current and match the action of the marabou. If you

Choosing Marabou

The term marabou refers to the original material used in salmon flies, large downy plumes from a marabou stork. Today, all marabou comes from domestic chickens and turkeys, and most of the marabou you see in dyed colors, other than very tiny feathers or black barred feathers, comes from large, white domestic turkeys. Any large bird has "marabou," usually on the back of the bird under its wings, and I have some gorgeous dark brown marabou that came from a turkey vulture who stayed with a carcass a little too long on the busy road in front of my house.

The shortest marabou feathers, called mini marabou, come from chickens and are suitable only for very tiny streamers and nymphs. Woolly Bugger marabou feathers, also called marabou blood feathers, come from under the wings of a turkey. They are shorter, fuller, and fluffier than other marabou and are the best material for most Woolly Buggers. The feather has a very thin, almost invisible stem, which makes it less bulky and easier to tie in. Strung marabou is slightly longer than blood feathers, typically has a thicker stem, and is best for larger stream-

ers and for winding on the shank like hackle, a technique often used for tarpon flies. It is usually strung on a long string for convenience and comes from the top of the thigh of a turkey near the butt. Select marabou also comes from the thigh of a turkey; it is longest of all and has the heaviest stem, making it perfect for very large streamers and saltwater flies. You can still use the longer strung and select marabou for smaller Woolly Buggers, but the tips of the fibers are not as uniform so it's tough to get a full, fluffy tail (plus you waste a lot of the feather).

All marabou is not created equal, and even in a good bag there will be some that won't be usable on a Woolly Bugger. Look for marabou that has no gaps in the feather and is full and fluffy, without the thin ends you sometimes see on it. If you want a very full tail, find two feathers that match in length and fluffiness. Snip the center stem from the tips of two feathers (if using select or strung marabou) and place the two feathers together. You'll notice some marabou plumes have a decided curvature. If they do, place the feathers together with concave sides facing each other and slide one feather up or back until the ends of both feathers line up.

Marabou is very easy to work with, much easier than dealing with hackles, quill wings, or hair. It stays right on the hook without rolling over the top and is easy to trim. The one problem tiers do have with marabou is that when tying it in, the butts of the feathers are often so full and fluffy that they become hard to manage and actually obscure the hook so you can't see what you are doing. If you have that problem, just wet the plumes slightly with fingers dipped in a glass of water and you'll be able to manage marabou like a champ.

■ Different types of marabou, from left to right: small chicken marabou, marabou blood feathers, strung marabou, and select marabou.

want to tie variations for different water types, you might tie some with very webby hackle for slow water and some with stiffer, glossy, dry-fly saddles for fast water (the webbier hackle gets pushed back along the body when retrieved in fast current).

Although there is only one true Woolly Bugger, the pattern shown here, today it is really considered a style of fly, and as long as a pattern has palmered hackle and a marabou tail, it has Woolly Bugger DNA.

■ OPPOSITE: Large Chilean brown trout taken on a Tunghead Krystal Bugger.

1 ■ Weight about half the shank of the hook, leaving about 10 percent of the hook shank free in front of the wire and 40 percent behind it. Start the thread in front of the wire, form a small bump, then hold the wire in place with your thumbnail while you spiral back to secure the rear end of the wire. Crisscross the weighting wire with your thread several times. Bring the thread back to the bend of the hook. Double a piece of 30- to 40-pound fluorocarbon over the hook shank so that a loop extends about one hook gape beyond the bend. Wind forward over the two ends, keeping one piece on each side of the hook as you wind forward. Trim the ends of the fluorocarbon even with the ends of the weighting wire. Coat the entire arrangement with head cement.

2 ■ Wind back to the bend. Tie in one or two pieces of black marabou above the foul guard with several tight turns of thread. The marabou should extend about one hook-shank length beyond the bend. Trim the marabou butts even with the weighting wire and wind forward over them. Wind back to the tail.

3 ■ Pick a black saddle hackle that has fibers just slightly longer than the gape of the hook in length. Stroke the fibers back toward the butt of the feather so they stand at 90-degree angles to the stem. Trim the fibers close to the stem for a short distance below the tip of the hackle. Tie in the hackle tip, leaving a short piece of trimmed stem so that you can make your initial turn. Strip the fuzz from a piece of chenille,

about half an inch from the end, to expose the two cotton core fibers. Tie in these threads as you wind forward to just behind the eye.

4 ■ Twist the chenille slightly and wind forward to just behind the eye. When you get to the tie-off point, secure the chenille with three tight turns of thread and trim it so that half an inch is left. Strip the fuzz from the cotton cores, then bind these under with several more tight turns of thread, giving you a secure tie-off point with no bulk.

5 ■ Lift the hackle upright and stroke all the fibers back toward the rear of the hook. Begin winding, angling the hackle so that the fibers all sweep toward the rear. After each turn of hackle, stroke the fibers back again and adjust the stem of the hackle by twisting it one way or another so that the fibers lie back. Tie off just behind the eye.

6 ■ Whip finish and apply a drop of head cement to the head.

Saltwater Flies

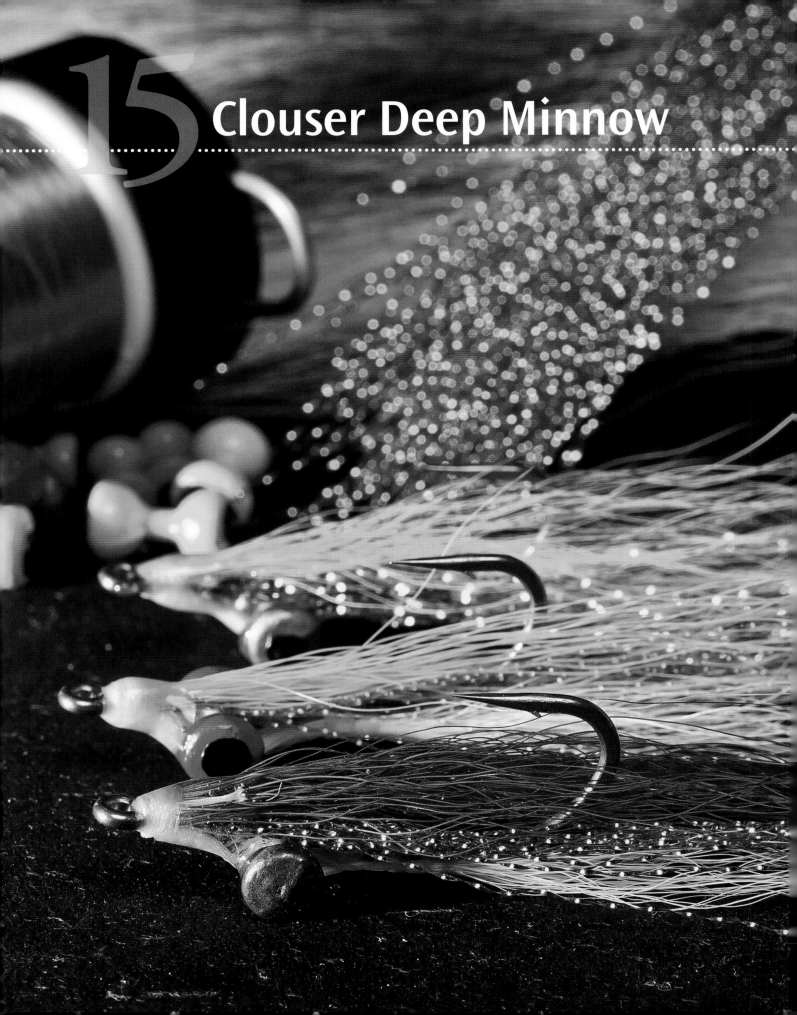

15 Clouser Deep Minnow

I n the mid-1980s, two innovative fly tiers were working on new patterns to imitate baitfish. Their efforts came together in one of the most popular flies in the world, a fly that Lefty Kreh has used to catch 96 different species of fish—in both fresh- and saltwater—around the world.

Tom Schmuecker owns Wapsi Fly Company, one of the best and largest suppliers of fly-tying materials in the world. For his own trout fishing—in the White River near his location in Mountain Home, Arkansas—he used large fur-strip streamer flies. He couldn't get the flies to run deep enough, and wanted to obtain the seductive jigging action that appeals to all game fish. At first he used bead-chain eyes, then later he began to fill the hollow eyes with lead. The resulting eyes were difficult to make and not very durable. Schmuecker loves to tinker with fly-tying tools and materials, so he developed a mold to make dumbbell-shaped lead eyes that could be lashed to a hook. Fly tying today would not be the same without his brilliant invention.

Schmuecker sent some of his new eyes to Bob Clouser, a small-mouth bass guide and fly-shop owner on the lower Susquehanna River, home of some of the finest smallmouth fishing in the world. Clouser had been experimenting with simple brown-and-white bucktails, crimping a split shot on the hook to mimic the action of a jig, a deadly spin-fishing lure for small-

Bob Clouser

Pattern Description

Hook
Standard saltwater, sizes 3/0–8

Thread
White 3/0

Eyes
Unpainted lead dumbbell eyes

Belly
White bucktail

Wing
Brown bucktail over six to eight strands
of gold Krystal Flash

mouths. The split shot flies worked great, but it was difficult to keep the shot on the hook. Clouser took one look at his friend's new eyes and knew they were the key to a successful fly.

Clouser began using the flies on Susquehanna smallmouths and other species with great success. One day his fishing buddy, Lefty Kreh, came into his shop before a smallmouth trip.

Clouser handed Kreh some of his sparse, simple flies. "Are they done?" Kreh asked Clouser when he saw how simple they were. Later that day, after fishing, Kreh came back to Clouser's shop and uttered two words: "They're done."

Kreh wrote an article about the flies for *Fly Fisherman Magazine* in 1989 and the word was out. The Clouser Deep Minnow is now used everywhere; originally developed for smallmouth bass, it has become the most popular saltwater fly in the world. It catches any fish that will eat baitfish, crabs, or shrimp, and I have even found trout-fishing guides with a box full of Clouser Minnows (most sheepishly admit it is their go-to fly when conditions get tough).

The Clouser is tied in nearly every color combination possible. The two most popular colors today are gray with a white belly and chartreuse with a white belly, in addition to the original brown and white. Like most flies that seem simple at first, there are tricks to making an effective Clouser Minnow. The first is to avoid tying the bucktail in too close to the lead eyes, as this makes the bucktail flare and causes the fly to

Pattern Variations

HALF-AND-HALF

Hook: Standard saltwater, sizes 3/0–8

Thread: White 3/0

Tail: Four to eight saddle hackles over about 10 strands of Krystal Flash

Eyes: Lead dumbbell eyes, usually painted

Belly: Bucktail

Wing: Bucktail, typically a darker color

ULTRA HAIR ALBIE CLOUSER

Hook: Standard saltwater, sizes 1/0–6

Thread: White 3/0

Eyes: Silver plated lead eyes

Throat: Thick, short bunch of red Krystal Flash

Belly: White Ultra Hair, tapered with scissors

Wing: Brown, olive, blue, or gray Ultra Hair, tapered with scissors, over 10 strands of silver or rainbow Krystal Flash

lose its streamlined shape. You should also avoid placing the eyes too far forward, as this makes it difficult to finish the head of the fly and again ruins the streamlined shape. Another trick is to make the central Krystal Flash stripe just slightly longer than the bucktail. Besides giving it a nice taper at the rear, the flash streaming out behind it adds action and sparkle to the fly. But perhaps the most important thing to remember when tying a Clouser Deep Minnow is to keep the materials sparse. The bucktail used for the wing and belly, when compressed, should be about the diameter of a wooden match. Too much material ruins both the action and the sleek taper of the fly.

Natural and Synthetic Materials

The rumors about the demise of natural materials in fly tying are greatly exaggerated. In the 1970s, when many new materials entered the fly-tying world, it was often said that the use of feathers, hairs, and furs in fly tying would soon be a thing of the past. But we're well into the 21st century and it would be very hard to tie most of the fly patterns we use without bird feathers and mammal coverings.

I remember a time 20 years ago when chicken hackle for tying dry flies was very scarce, with the supply locked up, for the most part, with a single large operation. The product developers at Orvis went on a quest to develop synthetic hackle, working with some top-notch plastics experts. In hindsight, this dismal failure was foolish from the start. Synthetically fabricating material with a thin yet strong and flexible stem and hundreds of very finely tapered fibers emanating from it is not something even computer-aided design could handle. It's not only the taper and microscopic structure of natural materials that is hard to mimic, but also the colors and textures, which are nearly impossible to reproduce with dyes (which turn every facet of a material into the same uniform shade). Evolution has a head start of a few million years on us.

Take one simple material—the bucktail used in a Clouser Deep Minnow—as an example. Each hair is strong yet flexible, with a finely pointed taper that no synthetic that I know of can match. And when the hair is cut from a tail, the shape of the whole bunch is naturally tapered, so the effect in a finished fly is a flowing, lifelike shape rather than the squared-off shape of man-made fibers. You can take a hunk of hair from a bucktail and tie it right to the hook to get a flowing taper. Getting the same effect with a synthetic fiber like Ultra Hair requires careful and tedious trimming, and the end result is nowhere near as sleek as bucktail. In addition, if you compare the solid uniform brown color of a Clouser Minnow tied with Ultra Hair to one tied with brown bucktail, you'll see that the Ultra Hair is a solid, bland tone, whereas the brown bucktail exhibits many different shades, which makes it a much better imitation of the mottled body of a baitfish.

I'm not implying that synthetic materials are not useful or welcome in the world of fly tying. We've been using man-made materials—hooks, thread, tinsel—for hundreds of years. I tie many of my Clouser Deep Minnows with Ultra Hair and other synthetic hairs, and they look fine and the fish seem to accept them eagerly. But Bob Clouser has been experimenting with all of these materials for more than 30 years, and his material of choice is still bucktail.

Bucktail comes with a beautiful taper naturally. To get the same taper from a synthetic like Ultra Hair requires a lot of tedious trimming and the finished shape is still not as subtle.

1 ■ Wind a bump of thread in the middle of the hook shank. Advance the thread a few turns toward the eye of the hook.

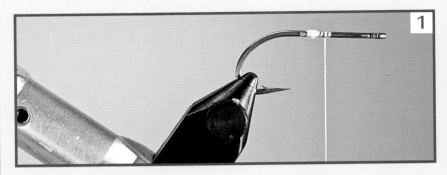

2 ■ Lay a pair of lead eyes on top of the hook shank. First, secure them in place with about eight figure-eight wraps. Make sure these wraps are very tight with constant tension. Next, make an equal number of wraps in a circular horizontal motion between the hook shank and the eyes. Make sure that you apply very tight pressure at all angles (front, back, far side, near side) to firmly lock the eyes in place. Don't rely on epoxy added later; without very firm thread wraps, the eyes will spin around the hook.

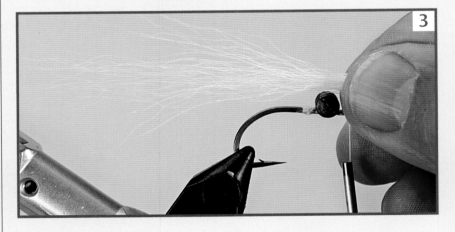

3 ■ Advance the thread to a point halfway between the eye of the hook and the lead eyes. Cut a sparse bunch of white bucktail, and remove the fuzz and short fibers from the base of the hair. Measure it against the fly so that the bucktail is two to two-and-a-half times the length of the hook shank. Pinch the bucktail at the point that gives you the right length and cut the ends of the bucktail square.

4 ■ Hold the bucktail at a 45-degree angle over the hook shank. Make two loose turns of thread to gather it, then make several very tight turns, wrapping toward the eye of the hook.

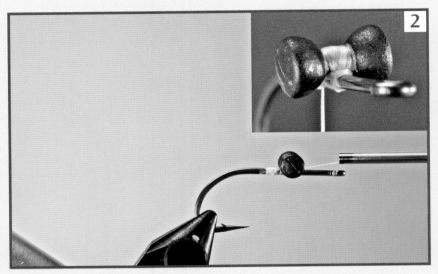

5 ■ Bring the thread behind the eyes and bump of thread. While lifting the bucktail up again at a 45-degree angle, make three tight wraps over the bucktail, spiral backward a few turns, and then return the thread to the point in front of the eyes where the white bucktail was tied in.

6 ■ Turn the fly over in the vise or rotate your vise so the hook is upside down. Cut a long length of six to eight fibers of Krystal Flash, wetting it to make it easier to handle, and measure it so that it is slightly longer than the bucktail. Holding this point in your fingers, fold the Krystal Flash over and cut the other end so that it is about one-third shorter than the length of the long side. Fold the Krystal Flash over the thread, slide it to the top of the hook shank, and secure it in place.

7 ■ Remove the hook from the vise and make sure the Krystal Flash is along the midpoint of the hook and straddles the bend. Put the fly back in the vise. Measure and cut a length of brown bucktail in the same way you did the white bucktail and tie it in on top of the Krystal Flash. Wind a tight, neat head and whip finish.

8 ■ Finish the head with your cement of choice. Epoxy is the best and most durable. When cementing the head, make sure you extend the cement back to the eyes, which further secures them and gives the head of the fly a nice tapered shape.

16

Crazy Charlie

The Crazy Charlie is the grandfather of most modern bonefish flies because it was the first bonefish fly to utilize bead-chain eyes—perhaps the first saltwater fly ever to use metal eyes. Prior to its development in 1976, most bonefish flies were relatively simple with fur or chenille bodies and wings made of nylon Fishair or bucktail. Flies like Chico Fernandez's Bonefish Special, the Snapping Shrimp, the Horror, and other flies that came out of the Florida Keys were used for bonefish throughout the world. And although some bonefish flies with oversized eyes existed—like Nat Ragland's Puff, made with glass taxidermist's eyes—no one had thought to cut a couple of beads from the pull chain on a lamp and lash them to a hook.

Bob Nauheim was a California angler who fished with the legendary guide Charlie Smith on the North Bight of Andros Island in the Bahamas. One day, they saw some bonefish feeding on tiny baitfish, commonly known as glass minnows, and Smith told Nauheim that he had often seen bonefish chasing and eating them. Nauheim was familiar with steelhead flies that used split beads for eyes to help sink the fly, and both men went back home to come up with a fly that would imitate the tiny baitfish. Nauheim's first pattern—made from a tail of silver tinsel, a body of tinsel covered with monofilament fishing line, bead-chain eyes, and a splayed wing of two white saddle hackles—was an instant success. Not only was the profile of the fly correct for imitating glass minnows, but the fly also sunk quicker than conventional bonefish flies on deeper flats.

Smith kept saying, "Dat fly's nasty," and although at first Nauheim called the fly the Bonefish Charlie Smith, he later named it the Nasty

Pattern Description

Hook
Standard saltwater, sizes 4–8

Thread
White 6/0

Body
Pearlescent tinsel, overlaid with clear vinyl like V-Rib or Swanundazes

Eyes
Bead chain, plastic, or solid metal

Wing
Calf tail

Most popular color is tan, but white, yellow, brown, and pink are also used.

Charlie. Bob showed the fly to guide Jan Isely in the Florida Keys, who changed the wing to calf tail for his own fishing and had great success with it. Nauheim later gave a few samples to Leigh Perkins, Sr., at the time president of The Orvis Company, who took them on his first trip to Christmas Island in the South Pacific, where they were equally deadly. I remember Perkins coming back from his trip saying, "We've got to put that crazy Charlie fly in the catalog." This is the name that stuck. When I made my first trip to Christmas Island in the early 1980s, my box was full of Crazy Charlies of various colors and sizes. I don't think I ever tied on a different fly during my entire week of fishing there.

Randall Kaufmann, another early visitor to Christmas Island, later modified the pattern slightly, adding a flashier body and lead eyes for even deeper water and the Christmas Island Special was born. Not only is this fly a spectacular producer on Christmas Island; it is also the top fly in Belize for both bonefish and permit. The other major variation on the Charlie is the Gotcha, developed by Jim McVay for the bigger bonefish of the Bahamas. If you plan on taking a trip to the Bahamas, avoid a disappointed look on the face of your guide and make sure you arrive with a boxful of Gotchas.

Pattern Variations

CHRISTMAS ISLAND SPECIAL

Hook: Standard saltwater, sizes 4–10

Thread: White 6/0

Tail: Orange Krystal Flash

Body: Orange Krystal Flash, coated with head cement for durability

Eyes: Solid metal

Wing: Tan craft fur over the remaining strands of the body material
- The most popular color is orange, but tan, white, yellow, brown, olive, and pink are also used.

GOTCHA

Hook: Standard saltwater, sizes 2–8

Thread: Pink 3/0, thick and heavy at head

Tail: Strands of the body material

Body: Fine pearlescent Mylar tubing wrapped over the body

Eyes: Bead chain, plastic, or solid metal

Wing: Tan craft fur over a half-dozen strands of pearl Krystal Flash

Eyes for Bonefish Flies

Most experienced bonefish anglers will tell you that the sink rate of a bonefish fly is even more important than what pattern you are using. In most cases, the fish cruise along the bottom, moving at a steady pace, rooting baitfish, shrimp, crabs, and worms off the bottom. When it flushes something, a bonefish quickly pounces and inhales whatever tries to get away. Thus, bonefish anglers try to cast far enough ahead of a cruising fish to avoid spooking it with the splash of the fly hitting the water, but close enough to intercept the fish before it changes direction. The fly should still be sinking as the bonefish approaches; in shin-deep water the sink rate should be very slow, in knee-deep flats the fly should sink at a slightly faster rate, and in deep channels the fly should sink quickly. Also, when fish are "tailing," or rooting on the bottom in shallow water but not moving quickly in any direction, the fly should land very close to the fish but with a subtle entry, as the loud splash of a heavy fly may spook fish in shallow water.

We regulate the sink rate of bonefish flies with different kinds of eyes. The most common type of eyes, for moderate depths, are those made from hollow bead chain, which are heavy enough to sink the fly but not so dense that they plunge it to the bottom immediately, where it can get hung up on turtle grass, coral, or limestone. Plastic eyes, with neutral buoyancy, are used when fish are tailing or cruising in very shallow water. Lead or nickel eyes are very heavy and are used when fish are cruising deep channels, where the fish are not as visible and anglers must get the fly in front of the fish quickly before it moves away.

There are hundreds of patterns for bonefish, some marginally better than others for certain locations, but most of these patterns exist because fly tiers love to create and try new patterns. Problem solving is half the fun. In most locations, only one or two sizes of bonefish flies are needed: sizes 6 and 8 in Belize, Mexico, and Christmas Island, and sizes 4 and 6 (and maybe even some big 2s) in the Bahamas and Florida. All a fly tier needs to tie in advance of a trip is a few patterns in light (tan, pink, white) and dark (olive or brown) shades. The most important consideration is that each pattern should be tied with all three types of eyes.

Sink rate is more important than any other aspect of a bonefish fly. This Crazy Charlie has been tied with plastic (middle), bead chain (left), and solid metal (right) eyes. Over a light-colored flat, these might be the only flies you need.

A Bahamas bonefish, the inspiration for the Crazy Charlie.

1 ■ Wind a bump of thread on the hook about one-quarter of the distance back from the eye. Attach a pair of bead-chain eyes with a half-dozen figure-eight wraps, then secure the eyes by winding an equal number of wraps in a circular horizontal motion between the hook shank and the eyes. Make sure that you apply very tight pressure at all angles (front, back, far side, near side) to firmly lock the eyes in place.

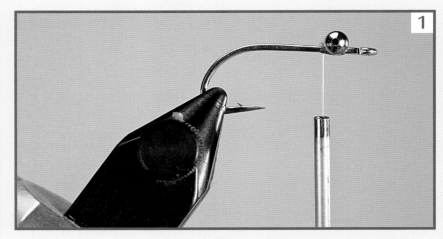

2 ■ Wind the thread back to where the hook bend begins. Tie in a piece of clear vinyl and wind forward, binding it under just behind the eyes.

3 ■ Tie in a piece of pearl tinsel just behind the eyes. Wind it back to where the vinyl was tied in with smooth, slightly overlapping turns. Reverse direction, wind forward to just behind the eyes, and tie off.

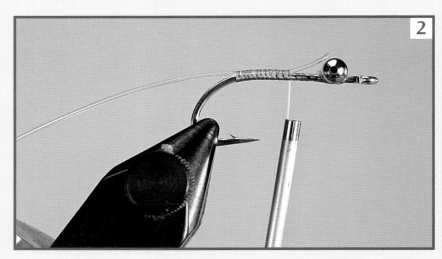

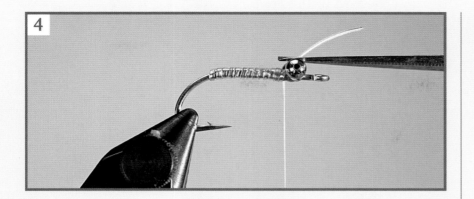

4 ■ Wind the clear vinyl over the body in even, non-overlapping turns. Secure the vinyl on top of the eyes so it does not interfere with the wing placement.

5 ■ Cut a bunch of tan calf tail about as wide as the gape of the hook. Remove all the fuzz and short hairs from the base. Measure the hair so that it extends to just beyond the bend. Cut the butts of the hair off square.

6 ■ Hold the hair at a 45-degree angle to the shank. Make two loose turns to gather the hair, then bind it under tightly, forming a neat head.

7 ■ Whip finish and apply a drop of head cement. Make sure a little of the cement seeps back into the eyes to aid in holding them securely.

17

Lefty's Deceiver

learned to tie proper Lefty's Deceivers the hard way. My first saltwater fly-fishing trip—which was for the giant bluefish that were abundant in the 1970s in the rips between Cape Cod and Martha's Vineyard—was with Captain Walter Ungermann, as far as I know the first fly-fishing guide on the northeastern coast. In those days, saltwater patterns for the Northeast were limited—you either fished a Skipping Bug popper on the surface or a Deceiver subsurface. A few people also fished the Gibbs Striper fly and Joe Brooks's Blonde series, but the Deceiver was really the universal fly. The poppers I bought; the Deceivers I tied myself, carefully following a pattern I found in a fishing catalog. When I arrived at the dock, Ungermann took one look at my Deceivers and said, "Whaddya think we're fishing for, Atlantic *salmon*?" My Deceivers were horribly spindly, with narrow saddle hackles and tiny pinches of bucktail that didn't even extend to the bend of the hook. And they fouled on nearly every cast.

I decided I would never make the same mistake again, and began to study the proper way to tie a Deceiver. At first it looks like a simple fly to construct, and it really is, as long as you follow a few structural rules. Lefty Kreh, the originator, said:

> It's really a style of fly and not a pattern, and you can modify it all different ways, but there are certain things you have to do

■ Lefty Kreh

Pattern Description

(Chartreuse and White Version)

Hook
Standard or 2X long saltwater hook,
sizes 4/0–6

Thread
White 3/0

Tail
Four to eight white hackles,
inside of which are six to 12 strands of
pearl Krystal Flash

Collar
Three bunches of bucktail, one white
on bottom, one white on top, with the
third bunch of chartreuse over the top

Throat
Short bunch of red Krystal Flash

to make sure it swims right and doesn't foul. You have to tie in the hackles at just the right point on the stem to get a tapered profile. And you have to make sure the bucktail goes past the bend, so it blends into the tapers of the feathers, so you get a baitfish shape and so the feathers don't wrap around the bend of the hook.

Kreh started saltwater fly fishing in the late 1950s on the eastern shore of Maryland. He and a fishing buddy named Tom Cofield used to watch commercial fishermen shovel piles of discarded crab pieces into the water, which attracted both striped bass and smaller baitfish in hordes. They wanted a fly that had more action in the water than what was popular in those days, and at first tried an all-white fly with a chenille body and saddle-hackle wings. The fly fouled too much, as the skinny saddle hackles would wrap around the bend of the hook, making the fly pinwheel through the water— a sure way to make fish turn away.

Then Kreh got the idea to put the feathers at the end of the fly and use a collar of bucktail to give it shape and keep it from fouling, as well as allowing the fly to be picked up and cast with a minimum of disturbance. The original all-white Deceiver proved to be an excellent baitfish imitation and Kreh soon began to use it beyond the eastern shore. In 1965, Kreh moved to Miami and discovered that a flashy material called Mylar was being used by tier and reel manufacturer Mac McChristian, who was famous for the legendary Seamaster reel. Kreh added a Mylar body and pieces of the same tinsel along the sides of the fly, added a red throat, which he believed was an "attack trigger," and also gave the fly a dark back made from several strands of peacock herl. He now leaves off the fragile tinsel body and peacock herl, but still uses a red throat (although he now makes it from red Krystal Flash instead of hackle fibers). In experimenting with the fly, he also found that the red throat should be short; it should be the merest suggest of red, and if it's too long, the fly will not be as effective.

The original Deceiver did not have eyes, but Kreh soon found that the addition of eyes made it a more effective fly, especially in clear water. At first he painted them on with lacquer, but he now uses stick-on eyes covered by a layer of epoxy, which produces an almost indestructible fly.

■ An original Deceiver tied by Lefty Kreh in the 1970s. He no longer uses tinsel for the body or along the edges of the tail, and he now adds eyes for clear water.

Kreh explained more about the possible variations for this fly:

You can tie the thing in almost any size and color combination. You can make a big, thick grocery fly for offshore or stripers feeding on herring, or you can make them slim and sparse for imitating slim baitfish like a sand eel. Just vary the size of the feathers and the amount of bucktail you put on it. The original all-white is still one of the most effective variations, but the top one is probably chartreuse and white.

For a mottled, sparse variation that is good in clear water, the Cockroach Deceiver, which borrows its color palette from the Cockroach tarpon fly, is excellent, especially in places where baitfish and other prey have horizontal barring and darker colors. I have also had great luck with an all-black Deceiver, for night fishing and for fishing discolored water. And the Deceiver is not just a baitfish imitation. With its full collar and streaming tails, it looks a lot like a fleeing squid, and when fish are feeding on squid, the Deceiver is one of the first flies anglers will try. My favorite variation is nearly all-white with an olive back; many of the baitfish I see in northeastern waters—like sand eels, silversides, and anchovies—have a dark green back.

The Deceiver is still my "if I only had one saltwater fly to use" pattern. It's perhaps the most versatile all-purpose fly in an angler's arsenal, and I've caught stripers, bluefish, bonito, false albacore, redfish, snook, bonefish, tarpon, barracuda, and sharks with it. Lefty Kreh has caught many more species all over the world on the Deceiver. It's truly amazing that a fly developed 50 years ago is still one of the most effective ones today, and that the basic pattern has remained relatively unchanged over all those years.

Pattern Variations

BLACK LEFTY'S DECEIVER

Hook: Standard or 2X long saltwater hook, sizes 4/0–6

Thread: Black 3/0

Tail: Four to eight black hackles, inside of which are six to 12 strands of pearl Krystal Flash

Collar: Two bunches of black bucktail, one on the bottom and one on top

Throat: Short bunch of red Krystal Flash

COCKROACH LEFTY'S DECEIVER

Hook: Standard or 2X long saltwater hook, sizes 4/0–6

Thread: Black 3/0

Tail: Four to eight grizzly hackles, usually tied splayed out, inside of which are a few strands of copper Flashabou and a few strands of pearl Krystal Flash

Collar: Two bunches of gray squirrel tail, one on the bottom and one on the top

Throat: Short bunch of red Krystal Flash

Hackles for Saltwater Flies

Selecting hackles for a Deceiver, or any saltwater fly that uses hackles, is not as simple as you might think. The same care that one would use in selecting hackles for dry flies has to be used for saltwater hackles as well. With big, long saddle hackles, there is a temptation to just tie the feather in at a different spot to get a shorter or longer fly, but approaching it this way is a sure path to a fly that doesn't look or swim right and fouls around the hook bend when cast.

If you look at a hackle, whether it's a saddle hackle or neck hackle, you'll see a point where the web in the center of the feather reaches the ends of the fibers. Shortly after that point, the web looks like fuzzy down. If you examine a hackle carefully, you'll also see that the stem of the feather greatly increases in diameter at this point. To tie a proper Deceiver or tarpon fly, this is the point you should use as the tie-in point. The hackle near the bend is still enough to keep from fouling, but the hackle beyond that point is more flexible, so the trailing part wiggles in the water like the fins of a baitfish or the tentacles of a squid. Too much of the webby stem extending beyond a fly is not a big problem (although you won't get as nice of a taper on the finished fly), but if the feather is tied in too short and the thinner stem protrudes near the bend of the hook, the feathers will not be substantial enough to hold their shape. Tying in a thin stem also makes it difficult to get the feathers to align properly because the thin stems tend to roll onto their sides.

Saddle hackles have beautiful baitfishlike shapes, but you get stuck with feathers that can only tie one length of the fly, unless you vary the shank length of the hook, and even by doing that you won't gain much. It doesn't matter whether you buy saddle hackle loose, strung, or on a full cape— even a full hackle cape seldom has hackles that vary much in length or shape. Happily, though, most saddle hackles are perfect for size 2 through 2/0 hooks and flies from three to four inches in length, which are the most popular sizes anyway.

If you tie very large or very small flies, it pays to invest in some saltwater neck capes. These are large capes with big feathers, not suitable for tying dry flies, but perfect for tying saltwater flies. Fly tiers who make tarpon flies have long used neck hackles, not only because they can get wider feathers in a great variety of sizes from a single cape, but also because neck hackles have stiffer stems than saddles. Although Deceivers tied with neck hackles won't have quite the same wiggle at the back end, the thicker stems on neck hackles make flies tied from these feathers almost foolproof, and if a wider profile is needed to imitate a big fly like a herring or menhaden (bunker), neck hackles make the perfect Deceiver.

■ The fly on the left was made with strung saddle hackles, which give a beautiful slim shape, but you are really stuck with one length for the fly. The two flies on the right were both tied from the white hackle cape above them, showing how a large neck hackle cape offers a wide variety of sizes.

TYING: LEFTY'S DECEIVER

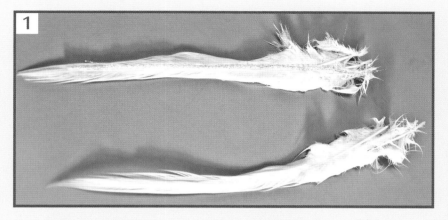

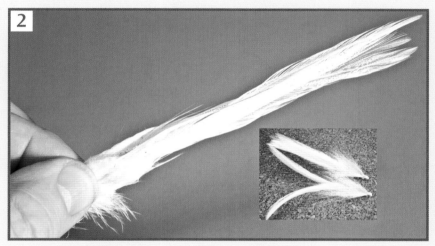

1 ■ Select four to eight hackles of an even number, separating them into two bunches. Place the two bunches on a flat surface so that the concave side of each bunch is facing in one direction. Wet both bunches with saliva or water to keep them together. Get about a half-dozen pieces of pearl Krystal Flash, wet them as well, and place them along the center line of one bunch of hackles. The Krystal Flash should extend almost to the tip ends of the hackles.

2 ■ Place the bunches of hackles together so that sides with like curvature face each other. For a slimmer fly that does not move as much water, place concave sides together (top fly in the inset shot). For a wider fly that moves more water, place the convex sides together (bottom fly in the inset shot).

3 ■ Line the hackle assembly up along the shank of the hook. The tie-in point should be where the hackles first become all web. Take a half-dozen very tight wraps over the hackles, pinching the sides of the hook as you tighten so the hackles stay lined up on top of the hook. Wrap forward about halfway up the shank of the hook in close turns, binding down as much web as you can.

4 ■ At this point, trim the butt ends of the hackles on a slight angle, leaving about one-quarter of the hook shank for the collar and head of the fly. Then, wrap thread forward completely over the butts of the hackles. Trim any long pieces of web and then wrap back and forth over the shank until the body is relatively smooth. It doesn't have to be perfect since the body won't really show in a finished fly. Whip finish.

5 ▪ Coat the body of the fly with the quick-drying cement of your choice. I like five-minute epoxy for a super durable, smooth body, but Sally Hansen's Hard As Nails, a clear nail polish, is also a favorite, as it dries hard and clear in just a few minutes. Super Glue will hold the body together, but it leaves a rough finish that I don't like. Don't overdo the cement on the body, especially if you use epoxy. The cement is just there to make sure the thread is not cut by the sharp teeth of a game fish. Be especially careful not to build up too much epoxy at the front head of the fly, as this will make the bucktail collar sit up too high and you'll lose the streamlined shape.

6 ▪ After the body dries completely, put the fly upside down in the vise, reattach the thread just behind the eye, and wind back to a point that is about one-fourth the shank length or about one-quarter of an inch on a size 2 fly. Cut a bunch of white bucktail about one hook gape in diameter when lightly compressed. Pull any extra-long fibers out of the bunch from the tip and thoroughly clean any small hairs at the base of the bucktail while holding it firmly about two inches from the tips. Tie in this hair so that the tips extend well past the bend of the hook, meeting the point where the hackles begin to widen so the fly has a sleek, tapered look. Don't use a pinch wrap. Let the bucktail wrap 180 degrees around the bottom of the hook. If it does not, move it around with your fingernail until it does.

7 ▪ Once the bucktail is in place, wrap forward very tightly to lock it into place, about halfway to the eye. Then, trim the end of the bucktail at an angle. (The easiest way to do this is to pull the ends of

the bucktail straight up and cut across them, which will give you a good taper. Trying to angle the scissors down on the bunch often cuts the thread by mistake.) Wrap toward the eye over this angle, and if the jump down to the hook shank is too steep, wrap thread back and forth in front of the bunch until the thread moves smoothly back up onto the bucktail.

8 ■ Bring the thread back to the initial tie-in point and tie in about a dozen strands of red Krystal Flash. The throat should be short, reaching only about one-quarter of the way to the point of the hook.

9 ■ Remove the fly from your vise and place it in the jaws right side up. Attach a second bunch of white bucktail, the same size as the first one, on top of the hook, ensuring that it encircles the entire top of the shank. You should barely be able to see the body showing through on the sides. It should be exactly as long as the bottom bunch. Trim it at an angle like the first bunch and make tight wraps over it to secure it.

10 ■ Cut a bunch of chartreuse bucktail as large as or slightly smaller than the white bunches and tie it in on top of the white bucktail. This bunch should lay on top of the second white bunch and not encircle the hook as much as the first two bunches.

11 ■ Stick a small flat decal eye to the middle of the head with a drop of head cement or Hard As Nails and let the cement dry. To finish, coat the entire head with a thicker coat of Hard As Nails or five-minute epoxy. Make sure you let the cement cover just a small portion of the thread collar to fully secure it.

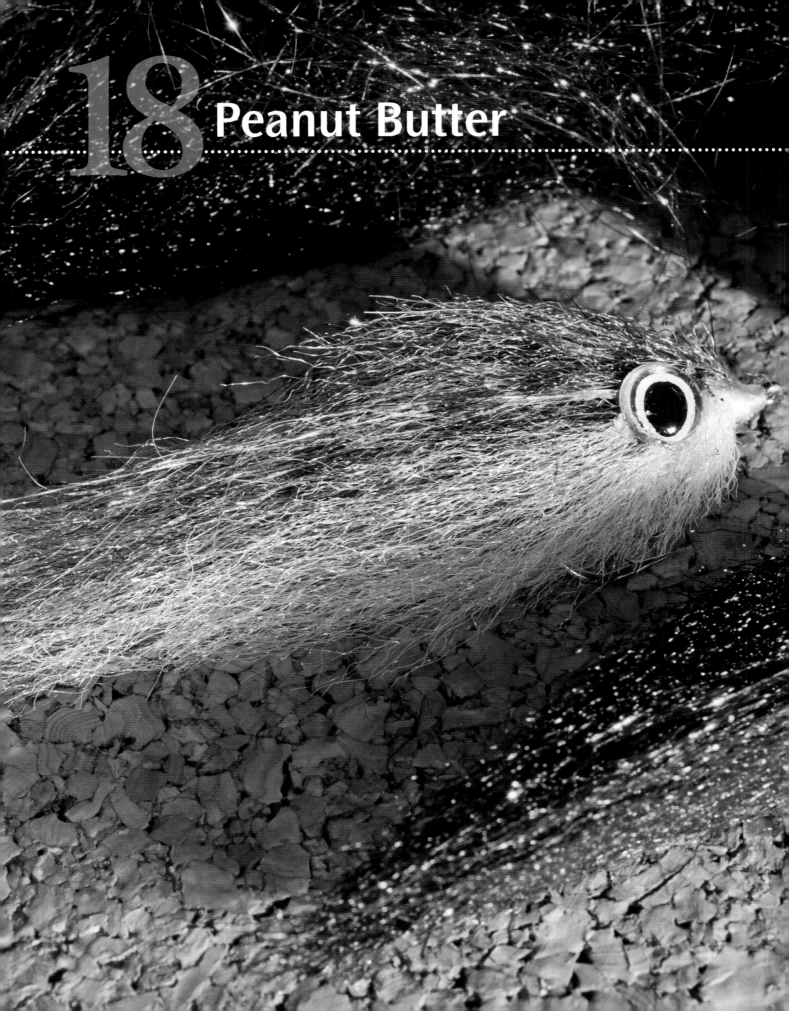

n the late 1980s, Enrico Puglisi fished for blue-fish and striped bass off the coast of Long Island. That part of the Atlantic Ocean hosts large populations of menhaden, or "bunker," as they are known to locals. At times, especially in the fall, fish feed heavily on young menhaden, also called "peanut bunker." Bluefish, false albacore, striped bass, and even bluefin tuna raid the shore-lines for these fish because they are rich in fats and proteins and are a high-energy food, perfect fodder for game fish about to migrate hundreds of miles on their journey south.

Puglisi was not satisfied with the bunker imitations available at that time, and felt that he could not get a wide enough profile with natural materials like feathers and bucktail. The flies fell apart after catching a few bluefish, the right colors of natural materials weren't available, and the flies still didn't quite mimic the wide profile of a peanut bunker. Puglisi, a chef by trade, began experimenting with synthetic materials and in time found a fine, durable fiber that could be dyed in any color. The fiber is polypropylene, which is hydrophobic, so even the largest, widest flies that use this fiber shed water (and weight) as soon as they are lifted from the water, an impor-tant consideration when you are trying to cast a six-inch fly into a stiff breeze. When I asked Puglisi where he found the fiber and what it was called, he glared at me and said,

Enrico Puglisi

Pattern Description

Hook
Short-shank saltwater hook (such as the Gamakatsu SC15), sizes 4–3/0

Thread
Clear monofilament 6/0

Tail and Body Accents
Red EP Sparkle fibers (Angel Hair and Lite Brite are good substitutes)

Body
Layered from black and purple EP fibers

Eyes
Large 3-D eyes

Stemmed eyes are preferred, but any large eyes will work.

"You think I'm gonna tell you?" I've learned over the years not to push a Sicilian when he doesn't want to answer.

Using synthetic fibers on a saltwater fly was not that unusual in the 1980s, when many new synthetics were making their appearance as fly-tying materials. What was new was the combination of just the right material, a method of quickly and durably attaching the material to the shank, and shaping the material to get a perfect baitfish profile, all without losing the natural flowing movement of the fibers when in the water. Puglisi's flies are elegant and his method of construction is brilliant.

Puglisi's method of tying is quick and efficient because there are no waste ends to cut. Materials are always layered on the hook, which not only makes the process quicker, but also makes the flies

When shaping flies like the Peanut Butter, it pays to use a pair of sharp, serrated scissors with much longer blades than typical fly-tying scissors. Cuts will be cleaner, and the long, flowing shape will be easier to obtain.

Pattern Variations

FLOATING BAITFISH

(Sample tied by Enrico Puglisi, shown after catching at least a dozen fish)

Hook: Short-shank saltwater hook (such as the Gamakatsu SC15), sizes 4–3/0

Thread: Clear monofilament 6/0

Tail and Body Accents: Pearl EP Sparkle fibers (Angel Hair and Lite Brite are good substitutes)

Gills: A bunch of short red EP Silky fibers tied on the bottom of the hook at the bend

Body: Layered from gray and white EP 3-D fibers

Eyes: Large 3-D eyes
- Stemmed eyes are preferred, but any large eyes will work.

MANGROVE BAITFISH

Hook: Short-shank saltwater hook (such as the Gamakatsu SC15), sizes 4–3/0

Thread: Clear monofilament 6/0

Tail and Body Accents: Pearl EP Sparkle fibers (Angel Hair and Lite Brite are good substitutes)

Gills: A bunch of short red EP Silky fibers tied on the bottom of the hook at the bend

Body: Layered from golden olive and white EP 3-D fibers
- After trimming, spots are added to the fibers with a brown waterproof marker.

Eyes: Large 3-D eyes
- Stemmed eyes are preferred, but any large eyes will work.

Note: This pattern can be tied from many different colors, and vertical stripes can be added instead of spots with the waterproof marker.

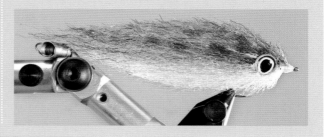

more durable because of the way the fibers are locked in. You could not do this with a natural hair like bucktail; when folding the second end around, it would have a blunt end due to its natural taper. To mimic the tapered look of natural materials (and of baitfish), besides trimming the fly at the end, Puglisi tapers both ends of each bunch by hand. The result is a fly with beautiful flowing lines that mimics a natural shape very well.

Puglisi's first Peanut Butter was a gray and white fly with pink highlights to imitate the shades of peanut bunker. However, the most popular variation today is the one shown in this chapter, in purple and black. I have to admit I shied away from this fly for years because I had never seen a purple and black baitfish, but after fishing with Puglisi and seeing his success with this color, I could not argue with the results. It may be that this variation is more visible in the water, or it may be that the fish just like the color combination. You could argue that these colors are more visible in deep water, but this variation is also the most popular and effective tarpon fly on the clear, shallow-water flats of northern Florida. Regardless, on numerous striped bass trips, the purple and black Peanut Butter has given me my biggest fish of the week, especially when fished deep on a fast-sinking line.

Dealing with Fine Synthetic Hair

Fine synthetic hair like the EP fibers that Puglisi markets can be nasty on the fly-tying bench. Add to that the Zap CA cement and the Goop that he uses to attach the eyes and you'll have a recipe for disaster. I recommend that you clear all other materials from your workbench and also put away any tools you don't need.

First, tape a length of male Velcro to each side of your fly-tying vise. Cut all the bunches you need to tie a fly and place them on the Velcro to keep them from flying all over the place. Then, place the remaining fibers off to the side where they won't get mixed up with the ones you plan on using. To get a length of fibers from the hank that comes in the package, separate as much as you need at the top of the bunch, twist it slightly, and then slowly and carefully peel it from the bunch. This will keep the rest of the bunch from getting unruly.

The right scissors make all the difference when trimming a Peanut Butter after the tying is finished. They should be extremely sharp, with slight serrations, and longer than any scissors you use for fly tying. Puglisi prefers scissors with two- or three-inch blades, as opposed to most fly-tying scissors, which have blades measuring an inch or less. These scissors are made for professional hair dressers and you should expect to pay around $100 a pair, but if you use them only for cutting fine synthetic feathers, they will last for many years. Shorter scissors will work in a pinch, but they do not cut as cleanly or evenly, and if you plan on tying lots of flies like these you'll be very happy with your investment.

There's a natural tendency to make these flies too bulky. You'll get a better shape after trimming and your flies will be easier to cast and have better action if you use about half the material you think you need for each layer. You'll be adding a number of layers of each color to the fly, and these add up quickly if you use bunches that are too large.

A fine-toothed comb or small brush (the kind with tiny round knobs on the end) is essential for both tying and fishing these flies. Mustache combs and flea combs have the right size teeth and work perfectly. The fly must be brushed out before trimming to get the right profile, and when fishing, the fine hair often gets mangled around the hook shank. A quick brushing will bring the fly back into shape before the next fish.

■ Both at the vise and on the water, you'll need a small comb or brush to keep the fibers in order.

■ OPPOSITE: The Peanut Butter, originally designed for striped bass, has become one of the top tarpon flies in Florida, especially in the purple and black color variation.

1 ■ Attach thread to the hook where the bend begins. Pull a long, sparse strand of red EP Sparkle fibers from the package. Catch the middle of the strand with your tying thread, slide the fibers to the top of the hook, and secure with a few turns of thread.

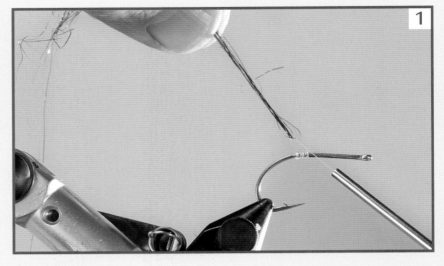

2 ■ Pull a small bunch of black EP fibers from the package. Cut a bunch that is about two-thirds the length of the entire bunch. Put the short end aside for using at the front of the fly. Work both ends of the bigger strand with your fingers until they are tapered and lose the squared-off shape. Fold the fibers in half to find the middle and secure the middle point to the same tie-in point as the EP Sparkle fibers. It should be slightly to the far side of the hook.

3 ■ Fold the front half over the top closer to the near side so that both tapered ends stream off the back of the hook. Wind slightly back over them with just a turn or two of thread to keep them pointing back. They should cover the entire 180 degrees of the top of the hook shank. Move them around with your fingers if they don't.

4 ▤ Turn the hook over in the vise. Grab a bunch of purple EP fibers and taper them the same way as the first bunch. Tie them in on the near side of the hook shank.

5 ▤ Rotate the vise back to the upright position and secure the other end of the purple fibers underneath the hook shank, again on the near side (which is now the opposite side of the first bunch). Tie a second sparse bunch of EP Sparkle fibers on top of the black fibers. Apply a couple of drops of Zap CA cement to the windings, then blot dry with a paper towel to remove the excess.

6 ▤ Divide a length of black EP fibers in half. Cut them and put half aside. Taper and tie one bunch on top of the hook shank as before, slightly ahead of the first group. Tie in a bunch of purple fibers on the bottom in the same manner as the first bunch. Tying in successively shorter bunches helps to get a good natural taper on the fly. Add another sparse bunch of EP Sparkle fibers on top.

7 ▪ Advance the thread on the shank slightly. Tie in the third bunch of black fibers on top of the hook. Tie in purple fibers on the bottom, but during this step, tie both ends of the purple on the bottom on each side so that you have twice as much material under the hook as on top. Tie a sparse bunch of EP Sparkle fibers on top of the hook.

8 ▪ Repeat step seven. If you are using a longer hook and are still too far from the eye, repeat again. Finally, tie one final small, sparse bunch of black fibers on top.

9 ▪ Wind a nice head and whip finish. Remove the fly from the vise and comb it out so that all the fibers layer nicely. Resist the impulse to stream the fibers back; the fibers should be combed out from the hook shank so they stick up, which will give you a sparser fly when trimmed.

10 ▪ Beginning from the back, trim the fibers into the shape of the baitfish you want to imitate. Shown here is the more traditional wide shape for herring, peanut bunker, or finger mullet, but you can make wider or narrower shapes as needed. Put the finishing touches on the fly by trimming from the front to get the shape you want.

11 ▪ Burn holes in the sides of the fibers for the eyes with a cauterizer, soldering iron, or heated nail. The holes should extend right to the hook shank.

12 ▪ Cut most of the stem from a stemmed eye. Put a drop of Goop into the hole you made and set the eyes in place. Gluing the short-stemmed eyes right to the hook shank, into this recess, will make them much more durable, but you could also use standard 3-D eyes.

13 ▪ Secure the windings at the head with Zap CA, head cement, or epoxy.

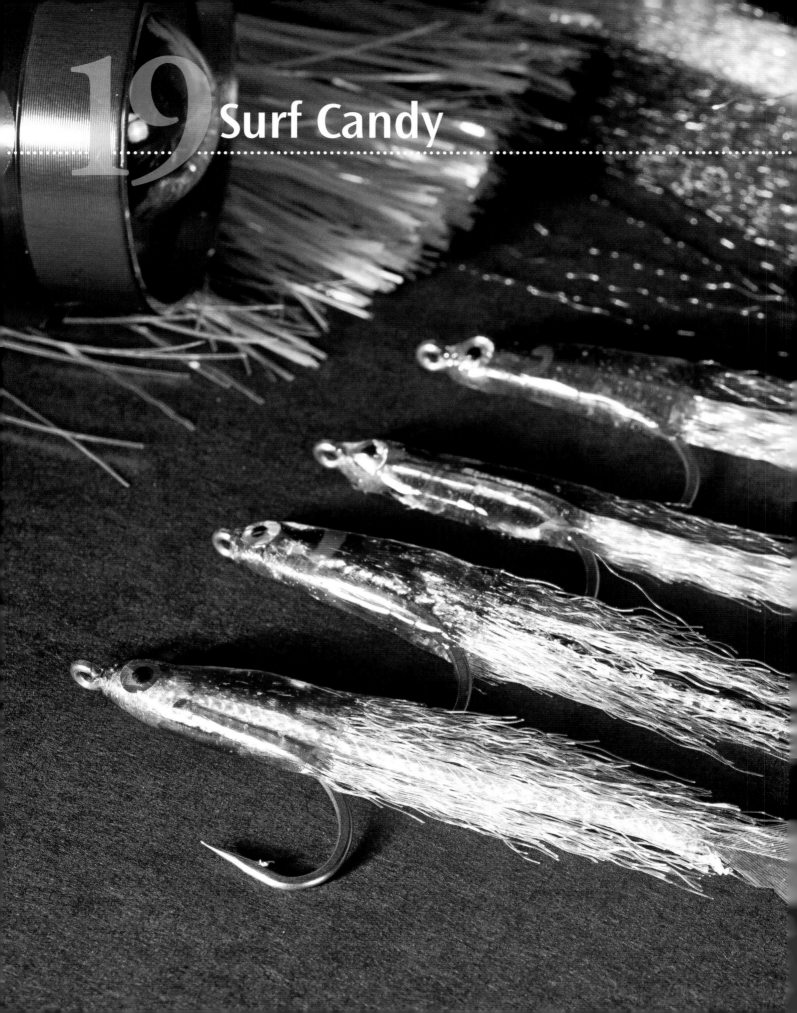

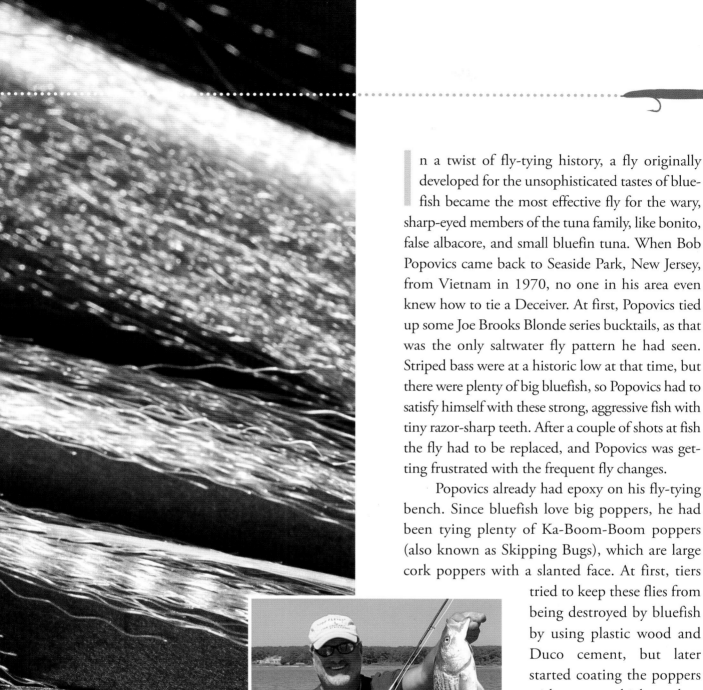

In a twist of fly-tying history, a fly originally developed for the unsophisticated tastes of bluefish became the most effective fly for the wary, sharp-eyed members of the tuna family, like bonito, false albacore, and small bluefin tuna. When Bob Popovics came back to Seaside Park, New Jersey, from Vietnam in 1970, no one in his area even knew how to tie a Deceiver. At first, Popovics tied up some Joe Brooks Blonde series bucktails, as that was the only saltwater fly pattern he had seen. Striped bass were at a historic low at that time, but there were plenty of big bluefish, so Popovics had to satisfy himself with these strong, aggressive fish with tiny razor-sharp teeth. After a couple of shots at fish the fly had to be replaced, and Popovics was getting frustrated with the frequent fly changes.

Popovics already had epoxy on his fly-tying bench. Since bluefish love big poppers, he had been tying plenty of Ka-Boom-Boom poppers (also known as Skipping Bugs), which are large cork poppers with a slanted face. At first, tiers tried to keep these flies from being destroyed by bluefish by using plastic wood and Duco cement, but later started coating the poppers with epoxy, which made a much more durable fly. "I just started with bucktail and epoxy and kept going. The first ones were ugly, but they sure worked. They had no

Bob Popovics

Pattern Description

Hook
Standard saltwater hook, sizes 6–2/0

Thread
Clear monofilament, size G

Belly
White Ultra Hair or Super Hair

Flash Stripe
Pearl Flashabou or similar, depending on effect and color desired

Back
Ultra Hair or Super Hair in darker color to imitate back of baitfish, typically tan, brown, olive, or chartreuse

Resin Overlay
Epoxy, blue light-cured, or UV-cured clear resin

Eyes
Flat stick-on eyes

Gill Slash
Line made with red waterproof marker

eyes and no flash and nobody else even wanted to know how to tie them because they looked so crude," Popovics said.

To get more translucency in his flies, Popovics began substituting polar bear hair for bucktail due to its glassy fibers, but polar bear was expensive and hard to obtain. A few years earlier, the International Agreement on the Conservation of Polar Bears had made it illegal to sell "the skins and other items of value" from polar bears, and any hair a fly tier could obtain had to be documented as sold before 1973.

In 1983, Ed Jaworowski brought Popovics a new synthetic material called Ultra Hair, which is made from translucent, slightly crinkled nylon fibers. "It looked like polar bear and I could really tie something that looked like rain bait," said Popovics. "And the new flies never fouled. In 1988, the Surf Candy was written up in *Fly Tyer* magazine and it really took off. People discovered the flies were killers for bonito and false albacore, which had always been hard to catch."

Popovics's first Surf Candy flies were tied with white thread and had no eyes or gill markings. He later switched to clear monofilament thread, which completely disappears when coated with epoxy, and added realistic eyes and gill markings. He even developed what he calls the Full-Dress Surf Candy, which adds a realistic body of Mylar tubing with a forked tail made from a slip of hackle feather. These additional accoutrements probably didn't add much to the effectiveness of the flies, but they did make them

■ The Surf Candy has become one of the top flies for Atlantic bonito (shown here) and its relative, the little tunny.

Pattern Variations

DEEP CANDY

Hook: Standard saltwater hook, sizes 6–2/0

Head: Tungsten cone or bead, placed on the hook shank before the thread is attached

Thread: Clear monofilament, size G

Belly: White Ultra Hair or Super Hair

Flash Stripe: Pearl Flashabou or similar, depending on effect and color desired

Back: Ultra Hair or Super Hair in darker color to imitate back of baitfish, typically tan, brown, olive, or chartreuse

Resin Overlay: Epoxy, blue light-cured, or UV-cured clear resin

Eyes: Flat stick-on eyes

Gill Slash: Line made with red waterproof marker

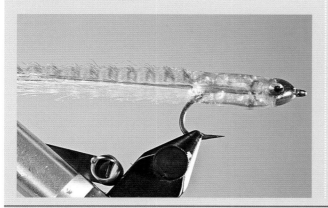

FULL-DRESS SURF CANDY

Hook: Standard saltwater hook, sizes 6–2/0

Thread : Clear monofilament, size G

Belly: White Ultra Hair or Super Hair

Flash Stripe: Heavy (about 20-pound) monofilament, small-diameter Mylar tubing, and hackle feather

- Tie a hackle feather trimmed to a chevron shape to a piece of heavy monofilament, then place a drop of Super Glue or head cement at the end of a piece of thin Mylar tubing and place the hackle tip "tail" and monofilament inside the Mylar after the thread core is removed. Tie the entire arrangement to the hook shank before tying on the hair for the belly or back.

Back: Ultra Hair or Super Hair in darker color to imitate back of baitfish, typically tan, brown, olive, or chartreuse

Resin Overlay: Epoxy, blue light-cured, or UV-cured clear resin

Eyes: Flat stick-on eyes

Gill Slash: Line made with red waterproof marker

look very sexy on the fly counter in comparison to most of the other saltwater flies of the late 1980s.

You can tie a Surf Candy to imitate almost any baitfish, from a tiny one-inch baby sand eel to an eight-inch needlefish used for barracuda. Spreading the hair laterally just behind the eye as the epoxy is curing makes a wide baitfish, what Popovics calls a Spread Fly, and adding a metal bead or cone to the head makes a Deep Candy, a fast-sinking version.

I have a real soft spot for Surf Candies. They are elegant, durable, and fun to tie. After seven years of chasing bluefin tuna unsuccess-

fully, my first was taken on a small epoxy fly, a simplified Surf Candy that was tied very sparse to begin with, and that I had to trim down with scissors to make it even smaller and slimmer because the school bluefin were feeding on tiny anchovies. These flies have created successful outings out of frustrating times more than once. There is a dock inside Menemsha Harbor—where I love to fish all night for breaking striped bass under bright dockside lights—and the only fly these fish have ever taken consistently is a small Surf Candy, drawn back so slowly it's almost fished with no retrieve at all.

Using Resins in Saltwater Flies

There is no getting around it—working with resins is a messy process. The better you organize your workspace and the more methodically you approach the process, the happier you (and your spouse) will be. Plus, your flies will look better. First and foremost, no matter what kind of resin you use, make your flies in batches. Do all the tying and cutting for as many flies as you want to tie, then clean off your workspace and make room for the resin-coating process. If you have the space, it even makes sense to do your tying in one area and fly coating in another.

It helps to coat your flies by holding them in a rotary vise rather than in your hand, as you can be more precise. A clean dubbing needle is more precise than a dirty one already coated with head cement or epoxy, because you want the resin to flow off the needle and onto your fly smoothly. Bright light and magnification are also essential; even though saltwater flies are large, you must be able to see all the nooks and crannies on a fly you are coating, and having great illumination makes that easier. When I'm working with resins I use two tying lamps, one coming from the right and one from the left, so I can see any little spots that I've missed.

There are two basic types of resin coating: two-part epoxy and light-cured resins. Two-part epoxies are harder to work with; they require you to work very quickly to avoid the stuff suddenly setting up just as you are trying to apply it, which produces a gooey mess. But two-part epoxy dries very clear, it is less expensive, and it does not require an additional coat of clear nail polish or other finish once the resin has set.

Bob Popovics originally used five-minute epoxy, and he never used a drying wheel, a small device with a slow motor that rotates the flies while they dry so that any drips even themselves out as the epoxy is setting. Instead, he coated the fly, moving the epoxy around with a dubbing needle, and then rotated the vise slowly while he sat and watched the fly to make sure the epoxy distributed itself evenly. By moving the vise to one angle or another, he could even out any drips that formed. I don't have the patience to sit in front of one fly for five minutes, so I have always used a drying

wheel. The drying wheel does tend to make the bodies of the flies more round rather than the lateral compression you get by rotating them by hand (spending more time with the fly either upright or straight down so the sides don't get as much epoxy), but I don't mind the round shape.

I recommend that you mix a single batch of epoxy for each fly. I used to try to do two or three flies with the same batch, but I found I would either hurry too much and get sloppy or I would try to coat the third fly right when the epoxy set up and thus ruined the shape. If you really want to do a bunch of flies at one time, try 50- or 60-minute epoxy. You'll have lots of time to fool with them, and you can add each one to the drying wheel after you finish coating it. Good drying wheels have a nice clutch feature so you can temporarily stop the rotation by holding it to add a new fly. Long-setting epoxy like this takes a full 24 hours to be tack-free, but the resulting flies are super-hard and very clear.

The best way to mix epoxy is on a sticky note right under your vise, so your travel from the goo to the fly is short and any drips will fall back on the paper. You can move the note around if you have to, and when finished, you can just crumple it up and throw it in the trash. Also, when doling out drops of resin and hardener, make sure you get equal amounts of both and drop them close to each other. Having to move the epoxy across the paper introduces air bubbles, so keeping the drops close will keep bubbles out.

Epoxy dries best in warm, dry air. If your resulting flies are tacky, even after 24 hours, your epoxy might be old, or you might have mixed it improperly, but chances are the air was too humid. Let the flies dry under a lamp, in the sun, or near a heater. I remember a fishing trip on Martha's Vineyard when it was so humid we couldn't get our epoxy flies to dry, so we put them in an oven at a low temperature.

Bob Popovics now prefers light-cured resins. Light-cured resins are either cured by ultraviolet light or blue spectrum light. The light is held very close to the fly and moved slowly over the top, bottom, left, and right sides to make sure every angle is cured. It takes literally seconds for the fly to cure completely. Make sure you buy the right kind of curing light (they look like little flashlights) for the type of resin you want to use. Ultraviolet light curing requires careful attention because the rays do not constrict your pupils and can cause cataracts over time, but the lights sold are well shielded and with care they are safe to use. I have used both types and the only advantage to the ultraviolet cure is that the flies are less tacky after being cured.

You can get light-cured resins in thin or thick formulas, as well as what are supposed to be "tack-free" (they don't seem tack-free to me) or flexible formulas. The thick version is theoretically what you put on first, followed by a second coat of the thinner variety. The advantage of these formulas is that you do everything in a fly-tying vise and they cure instantly, so you can do a second coat and the top coat in a matter of minutes.

Bob Popovics uses the blue spectrum light type exclusively now, and he uses the thick version for both the first and final coat. "There's no stress, no fussing," he said. "I can put on a coat, move it around, get it in place, go have a cup of coffee, and then go back and cure it. It doesn't run, so I can put it just where I want it."

All of the light-cured resins I have seen leave a tacky, greasy finish, although some more than others. This can be removed with a paper towel dipped in rubbing or denatured alcohol (or probably even vodka). The resulting finish is dull and milky and does not look as nice in a fly box, but the fly becomes almost transparent when wet. However, most tiers add a final top coat with products sold by resin manufacturers, or just a clear nail polish like Sally Hansen's Hard As Nails. These dry in seconds and do not need special light to cure as they are solvent-based. Once the fly is coated, it is as clear and shiny as one made with two-part epoxy.

A drying wheel and two-part epoxy are shown on the left, while one type of blue light-cured resin and the required special light are shown on the right.

1 ■ Attach monofilament thread to the hook and cover the front third of the hook shank. Bring the thread back to a point about one-quarter of the hook-shank length from the eye. Cut a relatively large bunch of white Ultra Hair fibers (when held loosely, this bunch should be about three-quarters of the width of the hook gape). Measure the fibers against the hook at the tie-in point so that they extend about two-and-a-half to three shank lengths beyond the bend of the hook. Cut the fibers off square at the front end. (It helps to wet the fibers when working with them to keep them in place.) Lay them on top of the hook so that they extend almost to the eye. Take only two loose turns of thread over the bunch and let the thread hang. Then, with the thumb and forefinger of both hands, roll the fibers around the hook so they encircle the entire shank. Inspect them from all sides to make sure they are evenly distributed.

2 ■ Once the fibers are placed where you want them, bind down the ends with tight turns of thread. Advance the thread to the eye of the hook and wrap, making a smooth base. Wet a small bunch of Flashabou, cut it so that it is the same length as the first bunch of hair, and tie it in on top of the white hair.

3 ■ Prepare a bunch of olive or brown Ultra Hair, the same size as the white bunch. Trim the ends square and tie it in on top with tight turns. Don't let this bunch roll around the hook; keep it on top. Bind down the ends of the darker hair and wrap a smooth head. Whip finish.

4 ■ Apply the first coat of resin carefully and evenly. The more uniform the first coat the easier it will be to add the second and get a nice shape to the head. Start just barely

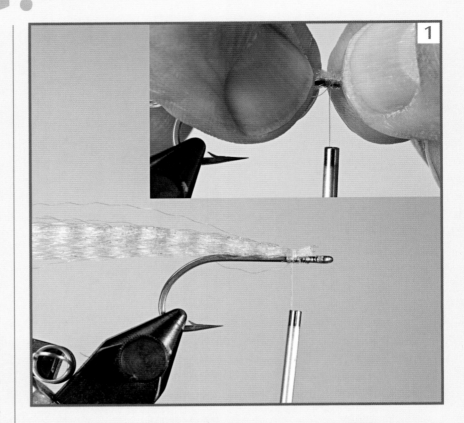

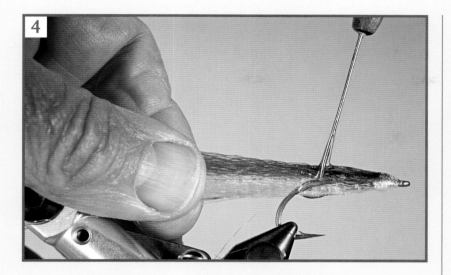

behind the eye of the hook and work backward, smoothing it out as you go. Make sure you work the resin into all the hairs. Hold the uncoated fibers beyond the hook with your other hand to make sure they maintain the shape you want them to be. Extend the resin to just beyond the end of the hook so the fly does not foul. By varying the amount you pull on the uncoated fibers, you can get anything from a narrow-bodied fly to one that is quite wide. Cure the first coat using the method appropriate for the type of resin you are using (see sidebar for more information).

5 ■ Grab a stick-on eye with a pair of tweezers and crimp it slightly, with the concave side on the opposite side of the printed eye. Attach the eye to the near side of the hook, as far forward as you can get it without the eye sticking out from the fly on the top or bottom. If you are using light-cured resin, the tacky surface will hold the eye. If you are using epoxy, add a tiny amount of head cement or clear nail polish to the back of the eye. Repeat for the far side, making sure the eyes are lined up.

6 ■ Add a second coat of resin. This time, take great care to make sure the resin is just where you want it before hitting it with a light or putting it on a drying wheel. Look carefully, as it is tough to see where the first coat left off and the second started, and make sure you fill in any gaps left by the first coat. If you are using epoxy, make a red gill slit line behind the eye before applying the second coat. If using light-cured resin, wait until the next step.

7 ■ If you are using epoxy, your fly is done. If you are using light-cured resins, however, first remove the tacky layer by adding alcohol (rubbing or denatured) to a paper towel and rubbing with relatively firm pressure from back to front. The fly will take on a milky look when it dries.

8 ■ Make the red gill slits, let them dry for a few seconds, then coat the resin surface with clear nail polish or head cement.

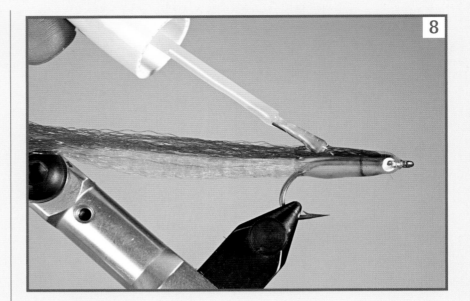

9 ■ Trim the wing, beginning at the end of the epoxy. Trim a few fibers with the tips of very sharp, serrated scissors, then move back, trimming a few more, tapering the wing until you get to the rear. It helps to take snips from the top, sides, and belly, then move back a little. Remove all loose hairs after each snip so you can see how your taper is progressing and make sure you are not inadvertently snipping the same fiber twice.

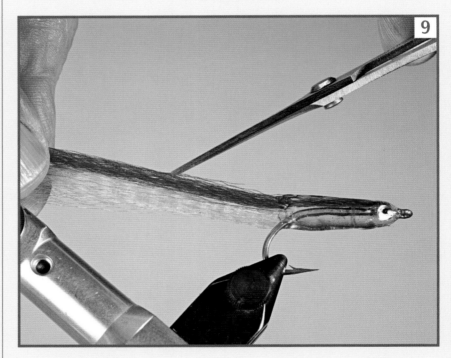

10 ■ This is what the finished fly should look like after trimming.

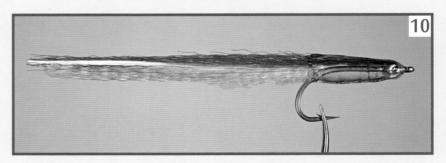

■ OPPOSITE: Although permit are more commonly caught on crab flies, they do eat small baitfish, and the author fooled this one on a small two-inch Surf Candy in Belize.

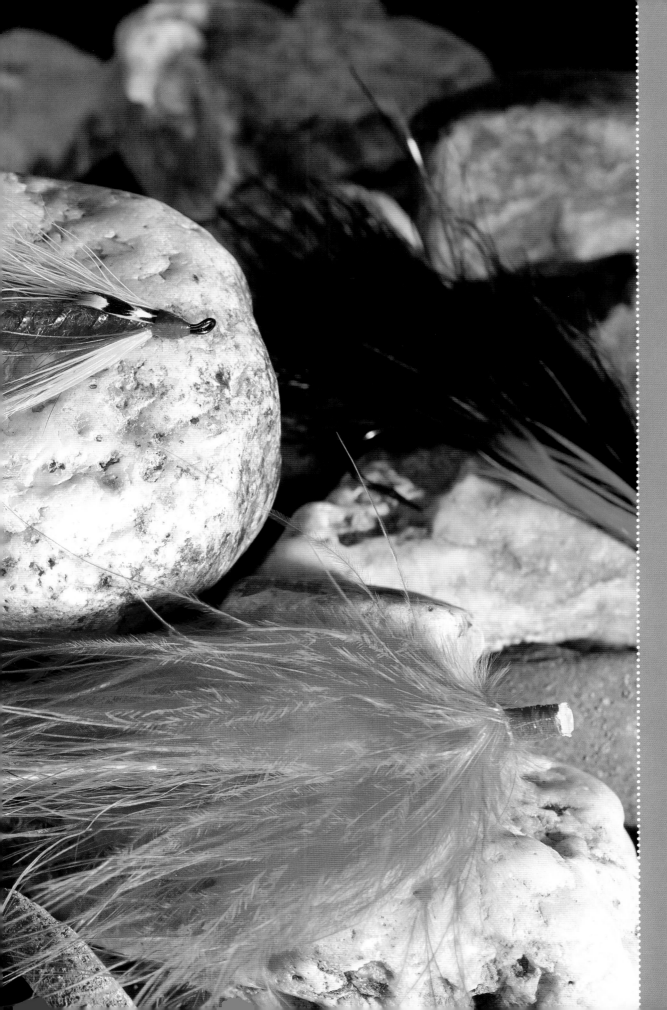

Steelhead

I t's hard to imagine a more poignant story of the development of a fly pattern than that of the creation of the Skykomish Sunrise, perhaps the first fly to regularly catch winter steelhead. Since the West Coast of North America was first settled, anglers have been catching the smaller, more eager summer-run steelhead on flies, but the big winter fish, under the cover of cold temperatures and heavy flows, were often beyond the reach of fly fishers. This was not a problem for early steelhead anglers. Unlike the salmon fishery of Atlantic Canada and Maine—where fly fishing was mandated by law and was mostly practiced by affluent fly fishers from northeastern cities—steelhead anglers on the West Coast have always been a more populist crowd, with experts from all walks of life switching between fly rods, spinning lures, or natural salmon eggs without giving it a second thought.

Ken McLeod was one of the most prominent pioneers of modern steelhead angling. He was an outdoor writer, conservationist, and tackle tinkerer who experimented with his own shooting head lines and stripping baskets long before they became popular with mainstream fly fishers. He was even instrumental in developing

George McLeod

Pattern Description

Hook
Standard up-eye salmon hook, sizes 4–10

Thread
Red 6/0

Tail
Red and yellow hackle fibers

Tag
Flat silver tinsel

Body
Red chenille

Rib
Flat silver tinsel

Wing
White bucktail, calf tail, kid goat,
or polar bear hair

Hackle
Red and yellow wound together

modern sinking fly lines, as he worked with Leon Martuch on the original Scientific Anglers Wet Cel lines—the first fly lines with a specific gravity much greater than water—which revolutionized winter steelhead fishing. But Ken McLeod, surprisingly, didn't tie his own flies.

According to Ken McLeod's grandson, also named Ken, his grandfather relied on his son (and the younger Ken's father), George, to create the flies he envisioned, patterns like the Purple Peril, another early winter-run steelhead fly that, like the Skykomish Sunrise, is still popular today. One January morning in 1936, father and son were driving to the Skykomish River and McLeod asked his son to tie a fly using the colors of the sun rising over the snow-capped Cascade Mountains, thus the mix of red, yellow, and white. That evening, George McLeod produced

a fly with the appropriate colors. The next day, his father baptized the pattern with three winter steelhead from a single pool, including a big fish weighing 17 pounds.

The fly caught on like wildfire. With the new sinking lines and the Skykomish Sunrise pattern, winter steelheading became more popular and productive. Both Ken and George McLeod began breaking records for the largest steelhead in the annual *Field & Stream* fishing contest, especially on British Columbia's Kispiox River, known for its giant steelhead. Between 1954 and 1975, 17 of the 60 largest steelhead entered in the contest were caught on the Skykomish Sunrise by the McLeods and other anglers—and another four fish were caught on a different McLeod pattern called the McLeod Ugly.

The Skykomish Sunrise remains the iconic steelhead fly even today, although the turned-

■ Original Skykomish Sunrise flies. The top fly was tied by the originator, George McLeod, and the bottom one by his son, Ken J. McLeod. The Sproat turned-down eye hooks have been replaced by traditional Atlantic salmon hooks by most tiers.

down eye wet-fly hook and high wing popular through the 1960s have been replaced with elegant salmon hooks and a lower, slimmer wing popularized by such masters of the modern steelhead fly as Dave McNeese. The pattern in these modern flies remains the same, but the sleeker profile reflects the more subtle steelhead fly, which sinks better and swims in a more lifelike manner—necessary to fool steelhead on today's heavily fished rivers.

Pattern Variations

SKYKOMISH DARK

Hook: Alec Jackson Spey or similar long-shank salmon hook, size 1.5 or 3

Thread: Red 6/0

Tip: Two turns of narrow oval silver tinsel

Body: Rear one-fourth should be orange floss, remainder should be red seal fur or substitute

Rib: Flat silver tinsel and narrow oval silver tinsel

Body Hackle: Yellow hackle

Wing: Bronze mallard, folded and low

Throat: Pheasant rump feather dyed black

TREY COMBS
SKYKOMISH SUNRISE

Hook: Standard up-eye salmon hook, sizes 4–10

Thread: Red 6/0

Tail: Cerise and yellow hackle fibers

Tag: Flat silver tinsel

Body: Fluorescent cerise floss over flat silver tinsel

Rib: Flat silver tinsel

Wing: White marabou, pearl Krystal Flash, and fluorescent cerise and yellow marabou
- Create this wing in three parts, each one shorter than the one below it. First, use white marabou over several strands of pearl Krystal Flash. Next, make a slightly shorter wing using white marabou. Last, use a sparse mixture of fluorescent cerise and yellow marabou to make an even shorter wing.

Throat: Fluorescent cerise marabou

Hackle: Fluorescent cerise, collared over the wing

Styles of Steelhead Flies

From the turn of the 20th century until about three-quarters of the way through it, steelhead flies were either oversized trout wet flies, Atlantic salmon patterns borrowed from Europe, or homegrown wet flies with hair wings and colorful bodies and hackle.

Today, it's hard to find a style of fly that is *not* effectively used for steelhead. They may be magnificent sea-run fish, silvery chrome when fresh from the ocean, but DNA shows them to be identical to the red-striped rainbow trout that stay in trout rivers and feed on bugs and baitfish all their lives. Because a steelhead grows up in a river at first and then feeds in the ocean for at least a year, by the time it returns to spawn, it may have fed on mayflies, caddis flies, stone flies, sculpins, mice, shrimp, salmon eggs, steelhead eggs, and a myriad of baitfish that live in both freshwater and saltwater. Thus, it has memories and reflexes that prompt it to eat nearly every variation of the standard trout fly, plus lots of attractor flies for which there are no matches in the natural world.

Steelhead fly anglers use nymphs, dry flies (usually big ones designed to skate across the surface), streamers, big articulated leeches, tube flies, egg patterns, and traditional Atlantic salmon flies. For many people, though, the biggest thrill of steelhead fishing is taking one of these explosive creatures on a wet fly swung in the current, either with a traditional, old-style steelhead fly like the original Skykomish Sunrise, or with one of the modern steelhead wet flies, some of which use fly-tying techniques originally developed to create Atlantic salmon flies, but with a unique steelhead aesthetic developed by the many great masters of steelhead fly tying.

The Skykomish Dark pattern developed by Steve Gobin takes the general colors of the Skykomish Sunrise and morphs the pattern into a fly that on the surface looks something like a traditional Atlantic salmon Spey fly, but with brighter colors more appropriate for steelhead. Other modern steelhead flies take the profile and colors of the old favorites and use flashy and more flowing materials for more sparkle and action in the water, like Trey Combs's variation of the Skykomish Sunrise.

The late 20th and early 21st centuries were truly a golden age in steelhead fly design. In no other area of fly tying do you see the vitality and cross-pollination of fly-tying methods from the Victorian era up to the present—with materials as traditional as a veiled bronze mallard wing and as modern as synthetic Krystal Flash and fluorescent materials—combining to produce an aesthetic that offers up flies every bit as gorgeous as classic Atlantic salmon flies, but with a pragmatic eye for how the flies swim across the current.

Variations in steelhead wet-fly design, clockwise from upper left: traditional Skykomish Sunrise dressing on a salmon hook; Skykomish Sunrise, tied in an Atlantic salmon style with a lower wing and more exotic materials like jungle cock, polar bear, and seal's fur; Skykomish Dark, tied in the Spey style; and Trey Combs's version of the Skykomish with Krystal Flash, fluorescent materials, and a staggered marabou wing for more action in the water.

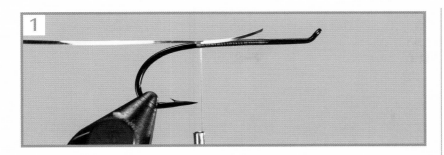

1 ▪ Attach thread just behind where the loop of the hook eye ends. Wind thread back so that it is hanging right over the point of the hook. Attach a piece of Mylar tinsel with three tight turns of thread, ensuring that the gold side is facing up. Wind the tinsel back over the bare hook for three turns, then reverse direction and wind it forward to the tie-in point. Secure the end of the tinsel with three tight turns of thread and trim both ends.

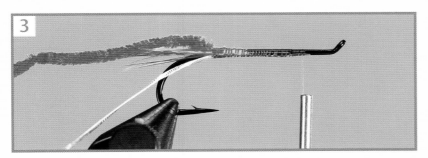

2 ▪ Pull equal amounts of red and yellow hackle fibers from large saddle hackles. Lay the bunches on the edge of a table or vise, line up their ends, and then pinch them together so the ends are even. Tie the hackle fibers in directly over the tinsel tie-in point.

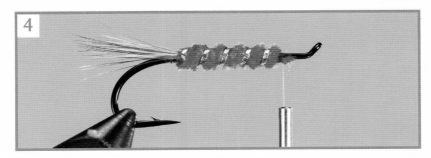

3 ▪ Strip the fuzz from the end of a piece of red chenille so a short thread is left. Tie this in right over the tails. Tie in a piece of oval silver tinsel underneath the hook shank and wind the thread forward, keeping the tinsel underneath the hook. Stop at a point about one-eighth of the hook-shank length back from the eye.

4 ▪ Wind the chenille forward and tie off underneath the hook shank. Wind the tinsel forward in even spirals, making sure that you take five turns around the shank. Tie the tinsel off underneath the shank as well.

5 ▪ Select a yellow and red hackle that has fibers that are about one-and-a-half hook gapes in length. Try to sort through the hackle so that the fibers on the two feathers are as closely matched as possible. Stroke the fibers of the hackles down until they stand almost at right angles to the stem. Trim the fibers on both sides of the stem on both feathers about one-quarter inch and tie them in with four very tight turns of thread. Trim the tips.

6 ■ Grasp both hackles together and pinch the fibers, stroking them back so that they point toward the bend of the hook. Make about three turns with both hackles at once, stroking constantly to keep the fibers pointing back. Each turn of hackle should be just slightly farther forward than the previous one; each turn should be touching, but not overlapping, the previous turn. Secure the hackles in place with five or six tight turns of thread and trim the ends.

7 ■ Wind forward to the eye and then back to where the hackles were tied off. Make sure the hackle fibers are evenly spread around the hook and that they sweep back at 45-degree angles. Wind the thread right up to the base of the hackles, but don't wrap on top of them, as this will sweep them back too much and the fly will not swim as well.

8 ■ Select a bunch of clean, relatively straight calf tail or similar fine white hair such as kid goat or fine bucktail. Remove all the fuzz and short hairs from the base of the hair. Even the hair in a stacker if the ends are not even. Hold the hair over the hook shank so that the tips extend to the middle of the tail, or about even with the end of the hook. Trim the hair square at this point. Pinch the hair on top of the hook and take a turn of thread over the ends. Make two or three additional wraps to secure the hair. Wind a small, neat head, whip finish, and apply head cement.

Index

A

Acrylic sealers, 19
Adams, 8, 46, 47, 49
Adams, Charles F., 46
Alf, Dick, 20
Allen, Leonard "Boots," 97
American Museum of Fly
  Fishing, 47
American Sportsman, The
  (television show), 69, 138
American (Troth) Pheasant Tail,
  8, 11, 108–115, 125
American Trout-Stream Insects
  (Rhead), 58
Antron yarn, 5, 82, 117, 119–
  121
Art Flick's Streamside Guide,
  57–58
Ausable River, 37, 68, 69, 81

B

Bahamas, 165, 166
Bailey, Dan, 18, 68–69, 138
Barnes, Pat, 97
Bass, 81, 137, 150, 159–160,
  181, 189, 191
Bead-chain eyes, 165, 167, 168
Beadhead nymphs, 112
Beadhead Pheasant Tail, 111
Beaverkill River, 149
Beck, Barry, 5, 149, 150
Beetles, 40
Belize, 166, 167
Betters, Francis, 81, 82
Betts, John, 82
Bighorn River, 45
Biot fibers, 126–127, 129,
  132–133
Black Gnat, 49
Black Lefty's Deceiver, 173
Blacktail deer, 81
Black Tunghead Woolly Bugger,
  151
Blessing, Russell, 5, 10, 150
Blonde series, 171, 189
Bluefin tuna, 189, 191
Bluefish, 171, 179, 189
Blue Ribbon Flies, 84
Boardman River, 46
Bonefish, 150, 165–167
Bonefish Charlie Smith, 165
Bonefish Special, 165
Bonito, 189, 190
Book Mailer, 5
Book of Trout Flies, A (Jennings),
  58
Brillon, Shawn, 5
Brooks, Joe, 17, 18, 138, 171,
  189
Brook trout, 137
Brown trout, 87, 88
Brush, William, 47
Buchner, Jay, 20
Bucktail, 69–71, 159–163, 172,
  176–177, 189, 206
Bucktail Caddis, 29
Bull elk hair, 90

C

Caddis flies, 10, 29, 31, 45, 88
Caddis pupae, 117–120
Caddisflies (LaFontaine), 82,
  117, 119
Calf hair, 50–51, 70, 72, 102,
  169, 206
Camp, Ray, 58
Caribou hair, 81
Catskill flies, 57–59, 63
Caucci, Al, 81–82
Chenille, 150, 151, 155, 165,
  205
Chernobyl Ant, 11
Christmas Island, 166, 167
Christmas Island Special, 166
Clouser, Bob, 5, 10, 159–161
Clouser Deep Minnow, 10, 151,
  158–163
Clumper midges, 40
Coachman, 67
Cockatush, 137
Cockroach Lefty's Deceiver, 173
Cofield, Tom, 172
Coleman, Monroe, 87
Comparadun, 80, 82, 84
Cow elk hair, 90
Crazy Charlie, 164–169
Cross, Reuben, 68
Crystal Bugger, 151
Cutthroats, 79–80

D

Darbee, Henry, 99
Dark Lord, 126, 127
Dave's Flexament, 19
Dave's Hopper, 16–18, 20–27
Deep Candy, 191
Deer hair, 21, 23, 25, 26, 29,
  31, 34, 80, 81, 83, 90, 97,
  98, 102, 118, 137, 138, 140,
  145, 146
Delaware River, 88
Dennis, Jack, 97
Dobsonflies, 150
Dry dropper, 46
Dry flies, 14–105, 204
  Adams, 8, 46, 47, 49
  Black Gnat, 49
  Bucktail Caddis, 29
  Catskill, 57–59, 63
  Chernobyl Ant, 11
  Coachman, 67
  Comparadun, 80, 82, 84
  Dave's Hopper, 16–18, 20–27
  Dun Variant, 59
  Elk Hair Caddis, 8, 28–35,
    90
  Fanwing Royal Coachman,
    68
  Foamulator, Black, 89
  Goofus Bug, 97
  Gray Wulff, 68–69
  Green Humpy, 98
  Grey Fox Variant, 59
  Griffth's Gnat, 36–43
  Haystack, 80, 81
  Horner Deer Hair, 97
  Improved Sofa Pillow, 88
  Joe's (Michigan) Hopper, 17,
    18, 20
  Letort Cricket, 18
  Letort Hopper, 18, 20
  Light Cahill, 49
  Orange Humpy, 98
  Parachute Adams, 44–55
  Quack Coachman, 68–70
  Red Quill, 56–65
  Royal Coachman, 67–68
  Royal Humpy, 69, 97
  Royal Stimulator, 89
  Royal Trude, 69, 88
  Royal Wulff, 66–77
  Rubber-Leg Crystal
    Stimulator, 89
  Sparkle Dun, 78–85
  Stimulator, 86–95
  Turck's Tarantula, 11
  White Wulff, 69
  X-Caddis, 31
  Yellow Humpy, 96–105
Drying wheel, 192, 193
Dun Variant, 59

E

Egg-Sucking Leech, 151
Elk hair, 81, 90, 92, 93, 97–98,
  100–102
Elk Hair Caddis, 8, 28–35, 90
Emergent Sparkle Pupa, 118,
  119
EP fibers, 182, 184–187
Epoxy, 163, 176, 177, 189–193,
  195, 196
Eyes, for bonefish flies, 167

F

Fanwing Royal Coachman, 68
Favorite Flies and Their Histories
  (Marbury), 67
Feather Tough, 19
Fernadez, Chico, 165
Field & Stream fishing contest,
  202
Flashabou, 150
Flashback Pheasant Tail, 111
Flick, Art, 5, 10, 57–59, 63
Flies (*see* dry flies; nymphs;
  saltwater flies; specific flies
  by name; steelhead flies;
  streamers; tying flies;
  wet flies)
Floating Baitfish, 181
Florida Keys, 165–167
Flue lengths, 39
Fly Fisherman Magazine, 150,
  160
Fly Formerly Known as Prince,
  125, 127
Foamulator, Black, 89
Full-Dress Surf Candy, 190, 191

G

Gapen, Don, 137, 138, 140
Gibbs Stripper, 171
Glass minnows, 165
Gobin, Steve, 204
Goofus Bug, 97
Goop, 182, 187
Goose biots, 127, 129, 132–133
Gotchas, 166
Grasshoppers, 17, 18, 20, 138,
  139, 141
Gray Wulff, 68–69
Green Humpy, 98
Grey Fox Variant, 59
Griffith, George, 37–38, 40
Griffth's Gnat, 36–43

H

Hackles (*see also* specific flies)
  for big dry flies, 99
  mixing, 48–49
  for saltwater flies, 174
  stripped hackle stem bodies,
    59
  wet fly and nymph, 128
Haily, John, 67
Half-and-Half, 160
Halford, Frederick, 10–11
Halliday, Leonard, 46–47
Hard As Nails, 176, 177, 193
Hare's Ear, 10–11, 125
Hare's ear fur, 30, 31, 33
Hart, Ron, 126
Hatches (Caucci and Nastasi),
  81
Haystack, 80, 81
Hendricksons, 57
Henry's Fork of Snake River,
  79, 82
Herters, 47
Hoffman, Henry, 99
Horner, Jack, 97
Horner Deer Hair, 97
Horror, 165

I, J

Impala hair, 68, 70
Improved Sofa Pillow, 88
Isley, Jan, 166

Jaworowski, Ed, 190
Jennings, Preston, 58
Joe's (Michigan) Hopper, 17,
  18, 20
Juracek, John, 79, 80, 82, 84

K

Ka-Boom-Boom poppers, 189
Kashner, Dave, 49
Kaufmann, Randall, 5, 87–89,
  91, 127, 166
Kenyon, Keith, 97
Keough, Bill, 5, 99
Kings River, 126
Kispiox River, 202
Kreh, Lefty, 5, 8, 10, 159, 160,
  171–173
Krystal Flash, 161, 163, 172,
  175, 177, 204
Kurtz, Ron, 112
Kusse, Ron, 149

L

LaFontaine, Gary, 5, 10, 82,
  117–120
LaFontaine's Deep Sparkle
  Pupa, 116–123
Largemouth bass, 150
Lauerman, T. L., 5, 19
Lead dumbbell eyes, 159, 160,
  162, 163

Leafhoppers, 40
Lefty's Deceiver, 170–177
Leonard Rod Company, 149
Letort Cricket, 18
Letort Hopper, 18, 20
Light Cahill, 49
Little Lehigh River, 150
Livingston, Montana, 18, 69
Loyalsock Creek, Pennsylvania, 29

M

Madison River, 79
Mangrove Baitfish, 181
Marabou, 123, 149, 150, 152, 154
Marabou Muddler, 138, 139
Marbury, Mary Orvis, 67
Martin, Alex, 47
Martuch, Leon, 202
Matthews, Craig, 5, 31, 79, 80, 82, 84
Mayflies, 29, 45, 57, 59, 69, 79, 80, 91, 109–111, 125
McChristian, Mac, 172
McLeod, George, 201, 202
McLeod, Ken, 202
McLeod, Ken J., 5, 201–202
McLeod Ugly, 202
McNeese, Dave, 203
McVay, Jim, 166
Menemsha Harbor, 191
Menhaden, 179
Metz, Buck, 99
Mexico, 167
Michigan Hopper, 17, 18, 20
Midges, 40, 45
Miner, Andy, 99
Mississippi River, 79
Moose hair, 49
Mucilin line dressing, 18
Muddler Minnow, 17–19, 81, 136–147
Mule deer, 81
Muskrat fur, 46–47, 55
Mylar, 141, 142–143, 172, 190, 205

N

Nastasi, Bob, 81–82
Nasty Charlie, 165–166
Nauheim, Bob, 165–166
Nipigon River, 137
Nymphs, 19, 90, 106–133, 204
    American (Troth) Pheasant Tail, 8, 11, 108–115, 125
    beadhead, 112
    Beadhead Pheasant Tail, 111
    Dark Lord, 126, 127
    Emergent Sparkle Pupa, 118, 119
    Flashback Pheasant Tail, 111
    Fly Formerly Known as Prince, 125, 127
    hackles for, 128
    Hare's Ear, 10–11, 125
    LaFontaine's Deep Sparkle Pupa, 116–123
    Prince, 8, 112, 124–133
    Sawyer Pheasant Tail, 11, 109–111
Nymphs and the Trout (Sawyer), 109–110

O

Oak-mottled turkey, 19
Ojibwa Indians, 137
Olson brothers, 127
Orange Humpy, 98
Orvis, L. C., 67–68

P, Q

Pale Morning Dun mayfly, 79, 80
Parachute Adams, 44–55
Paradun, 49
Patlen, Ted, 138
Peacock herl, 39, 41, 67, 75, 114–115, 130, 131, 172
Peanut Butter, 178–187
Perkins, Leigh, Sr., 166
Pheasant tail feathers, 20, 24, 110, 111, 113, 114
Pig's bristles, 47
Polar bear hair, 190
Polypropylene yarn, 21, 22
Popovics, Bob, 5, 189–193
Prince, 8, 112, 124–133
Prince, Doug, 5, 125–127
Puff, 165
Puglisi, Enrico, 5, 11, 179–182
Purple Peril, 202

Quack Coachman, 68–70
Quackenbush, Leonard, 68

R

Ragland, Nat, 165
Rainbow trout, 80, 87, 204
Ransier, Cathy, 5
Red Quill, 56–65
Resins, 192–196
Rhead, Louis, 58
Rhode Island Red stripped hackle quills, 9, 63
Richards, Carl, 47, 81
River Avon, 11, 109
Rocky Mountains, 18, 82, 88, 98, 125
Roosevelt, Theodore, 70
Rosenbauer, Brett, 5, 150–151
Royal Coachman, 67–68
Royal Humpy, 69, 97
Royal Stimulator, 89
Royal Trude, 69, 88
Royal Wulff, 66–77
Rubber-Leg Crystal Stimulator, 89

S

Saltwater flies, 156–197
    Clouser Deep Minnow, 10, 151, 158–163
    Crazy Charlie, 164–169
    hackles for, 174
    Lefty's Deceiver, 170–177
    Peanut Butter, 178–187
    Surf Candy, 188–196
    using resins in, 192–196
Sawyer, Frank, 11, 109–110
Sawyer Pheasant Tail, 11, 109–111
Schmuecker, Tom, 159, 160
Schoharie River, 57

Schroeder, Ed, 5, 126
Schwiebert, Ernest, 18, 82
Scientific Anglers Wet Cel lines, 202
Sculpin, 137, 138, 141
Seamaster reel, 172
Selective Trout (Swisher and Richards), 47, 81
Shenk, Ed, 18
Skipping Bug, 171, 189
Skues, G. E. M., 11
Skykomish Dark, 203, 204
Skykomish Sunrise, 200–206
Smallmouth bass, 150, 159–160
Smith, Charlie, 165
Smoky Mountains, 98
Snake River, 79, 80
Snapping Shrimp, 165
South Fork of Snake River, 79
South Platte River, 87
Sparkle Dun, 78–85
Sparkle Dun hair, 31
Spread Fly, 191
Squirrel tails, 138, 143–144
Steelhead flies, 198–206
    McLeod Ugly, 202
    Purple Peril, 202
    styles of, 204
Steelhead trout, 150, 201–204
Stimulator, 86–95
Stone flies, 87, 88, 90, 91, 112, 125, 126, 139
Streamers, 17–18, 112, 134–155, 204
    Black Tunghead Woolly Bugger, 151
    Crystal Bugger, 151
    Egg-Sucking Leech, 151
    Marabou Muddler, 138, 139
    Muddler Minnow, 17–19, 81, 136–147
    Woolly Bugger, 8, 10, 45, 137, 148–155
Striped bass, 150, 181, 189, 191
Stripped hackle stem bodies, 59
Summers, Bob, 40
Super Glue, 176
Surf Candy, 188–196
Susquehanna River, 159, 160
Swisher, Doug, 47, 81
Synthetic material, 161, 179–187, 190, 194

T

Todd, Helen, 47
Trey Combs Skykomish Sunrise, 203, 204
Troth, Al, 11, 29–31, 34, 35, 110–111
Troth, Eric, 5
Trout Unlimited (TU), 37–38
Tungsten beads, 112
Turck's Tarantula, 11
Turkey feathers, 19
Turkey quill, 19, 23
Turkey wings, 138, 141, 142, 144
Turle knot, 57
Tying flies
    American (Troth) Pheasant Tail, 113–115
    Clouser Deep Minnow, 162–163

Crazy Charlie, 168–169
Dave's Hopper, 21–27
Elk Hair Caddis, 32–35
Griffth's Gnat, 41–43
LaFontaine's Deep Sparkle Pupa, 121–123
Lefty's Deceiver, 175–177
Muddler Minnow, 142–147
Parachute Adams, 50–55
Peanut Butter, 184–187
Prince, 129–133
Red Quill, 60–65
Royal Wulff, 71–77
Skykomish Sunrise, 205–206
Sparkle Dun, 83–85
Stimulator, 92–95
Surf Candy, 194–196
Woolly Bugger, 154–155
Yellow Humpy, 100–105

U, V

Ultra Hair, 161, 190, 194
Ultra Hair Albie Clouser, 160
Ungermann, Walter, 171

Veniard's fly catalogue, 47
Vinyl cement, 19

W

Wapsi Fly Company, 15, 9, 159
Western March Brown mayfly, 57
Wet flies, 19
    hackles for, 128
    Woolly Worm, 10, 149, 150
White Marabou Muddler, 139
White River, 159
White Wulff, 69
Whiting, Tom, 99
Whitlock, Dave, 5, 17, 18, 20
Winnie, Art, 17
Wolf hair, 137
Wood duck, 61–63, 67, 68
Woolly Bugger, 8, 10, 45, 137, 148–155
Woolly Worm, 10, 149, 150
Wulff, Lee, 67–70

X, Y, Z

X-Caddis, 31

Yellow Conehead Marabou Muddler, 139
Yellow Humpy, 96–105
Yellowstone National Park, 112
Yellowstone River, 18

Zap CA cement, 182, 185, 187
Z-Lon, 31, 82, 84, 120